T0208325

Leadership Lessons:
Notes From and For the Journey

Jacklyn A. Chisholm Ph.D.

authorHOUSE®

AuthorHouse™
1663 Liberty Drive
Bloomington, IN 47403
www.authorhouse.com
Phone: 833-262-8899

© 2023 Jacklyn A. Chisholm Ph.D. All rights reserved.

No part of this book may be reproduced, stored in a retrieval system, or
transmitted by any means without the written permission of the author.

Published by AuthorHouse 09/26/2023

ISBN: 979-8-8230-0807-5 (sc)
ISBN: 979-8-8230-0806-8 (hc)
ISBN: 979-8-8230-0808-2 (e)

Library of Congress Control Number: 2023908772

Print information available on the last page.

Any people depicted in stock imagery provided by Getty Images are models,
and such images are being used for illustrative purposes only.
Certain stock imagery © Getty Images.

This book is printed on acid-free paper.

Because of the dynamic nature of the Internet, any web addresses or links contained in
this book may have changed since publication and may no longer be valid. The views
expressed in this work are solely those of the author and do not necessarily reflect the
views of the publisher, and the publisher hereby disclaims any responsibility for them.

Scripture quotations marked KJV are from the Holy Bible, King James Version
(Authorized Version). First published in 1611. Quoted from the KJV Classic
Reference Bible, Copyright © 1983 by The Zondervan Corporation.

Interior Image Credit:
Leadership Orbit #1 – Perspective and Role Traits (copyright #VAu001394551, 2019)
Process of Professional Role Formation – Cultural #1-9 (copyright #VAu001043419

Contents

Acknowledgments

First, I thank God[1] for the experiences that shaped this book and for my family—my mother, Sarah Johnson Betts (I wish you were here); my father, Leland Johnson (deceased); my husband, Robert; our daughters, Robin and Jennifer, and our grandchildren, Shanum and Yahya; my sisters, Karen and Barbara; and my nieces, Kia and Anaia.

I would also like to acknowledge those who have been and those who continue to be my biggest supporters, especially Dr. Jennifer Cochran, Kathryn Hall, Alexandria Johnson Boone, Dr. Ellen Burts Cooper, Charles Eduardos, and Katherine Harper; educators who changed my life, including Mattie Stephens, Lelia McBath, and Drs. Bert Holt, Robert Davis, Charles Callendar, Jill Korbin, Atwood Gaines, David Miller, and Lenore Kola; leadership mentors, including Richard Baznik and Terry Stewart; and others too numerous to count who influenced my life.

Finally, thank you for taking the time to read what I have learned regarding leadership. I hope that it helps you on your journey.

---

[1] Throughout the book, I will use the pronoun *He* in reference to God.

Introduction

My name is Dr. Jacklyn A. Chisholm. I have been privileged to hold various leadership roles over my career and am currently the president and chief executive officer of a nonprofit social services agency, the largest of its kind in Ohio.

The idea for *Leadership Lessons: Notes from and for the Journey* evolved in my mind for over eighteen years as I sought and was promoted to ever-increasing leadership roles. My initial effort to share what I learned was my blog (http://drjacklynchisholm.org), which became the foundation for this book.

My first blog post on April 23, 2012, was titled "It Is Worth It Because You 'Are.'" The title comes from the name of my company, It's Worth It Consulting, which I founded with my husband in 1999. The blog acts as an introduction to what I believe is my life's work: to pay attention for lessons that may be helpful to others. This blog details some of my most challenging times, which included physical and emotional abuse, suicidal thoughts, and divorce, and which eventually led to recovery, rediscovery, and renewal. In the blog, I write the following:

> This blog is my way of sharing what I've learned to make your journey, hopefully, easier. I've been blessed to achieve a great deal in my life with God's help: I left my first marriage and found my soulmate in the process, who became my husband. Robert is his name. … We have raised two incredibly gifted girls—Robin and Jennifer—who are the loves of

our lives and make us proud to be parents. We also have the most beautiful and brilliant grandchildren in Shanum and Yahya, who have added more to our lives than I can possibly say. I have also earned three degrees: a BA in medical anthropology, an MA in psychological anthropology, and a PhD in psychological anthropology with an emphasis in educational anthropology. And if all of this wasn't enough, God allowed me to become a vice president at one of the most recognizable museums in the world! Now, how's that for bouncing back!

I believe that it is now my time to share what I have learned along the way—the ups and downs—so that you, too, will know that there is life after hardship and heartache, even suicidal thoughts. Life is so worth it because you are!

So, if you're ready, let's take this trip together!

My goal, then as now, is to help people accomplish their dreams through education and personal investment. One of my two mottos is, "Dream big," because to dream big takes the same energy as to dream small. The other is, "With God, all things are possible" (Matthew 19:26).

My hope is you will find in the experiences and lessons I have learned on my life's journey something that will inspire you to pursue all that you are capable of and all that God has in store for you. It has taken me a lifetime to understand that I am worth it simply because I am—I exist, I am not a mistake. I am the image and the likeness of God; therefore, I am worthy to experience all the good that God has for me in this world.

As you might have noticed, I am a Christian. I make no apologies for this—it just is. Without my faith, I would not have survived to become the person who can share these lessons with you.

I consider myself like Hansel and Gretel, who left a trail of breadcrumbs on their journey into the woods so that they could return home. The breadcrumbs in this book are the lessons I have learned along the way that, I hope, will help you on your leadership journey.

I have been blessed to achieve a great deal in my life with God's help. My husband and I are now in our thirty-sixth year of marriage. Our children and grandchildren remain our best achievements. I am a Black, female, first-generation college student who has earned three degrees; was a vice president at the Rock and Roll Hall of Fame and Museum in Cleveland, Ohio; and am currently the chief executive officer of the largest community action agency in Ohio, with four hundred employees and annual revenues of over $150 million at the time of this writing.

In chapter 1, I begin with my background: the way I started my journey and the experiences that shaped me from early childhood to college.

Chapter 2 focuses on how I became a conscious observer who not only reflects on my experiences but also is willing to share the lessons I've learned with others when the opportunity presents itself.

Chapter 3 introduces my concept of the gravitational pull to and away from a different leadership level. I include definitions of the leadership levels and the changes in perspective that occur as you ascend to new levels.

In chapter 4, I attempt to chronologically list the lessons I've learned when it makes sense to do so. However, some do not have a chronology associated with them; rather, I consider them important for the insights they provided me.

Chapter 5 is devoted to what I call the *culture in leadership*, which is composed of conscious, and mostly unconscious, cultural factors that are part of any professional role an individual assumes.

I conclude my leadership lessons with a look to the future and offer resources that have been helpful to me in my journey.

With any good proposition, it is important to define your terms. So, let us start with what I mean by *leadership*.

Consultants Jack Zenger and Joseph Folkman, after surveying 330,000 businesspeople, identified a true leader as being someone who:

1. Inspires and motivates others
2. Displays high integrity and honesty
3. Solves problems and analyzes issues
4. Drives for results
5. Communicates powerfully and prolifically
6. Builds relationships
7. Displays technical or professional expertise
8. Displays a strategic perspective
9. Develops others
10. Innovates[2]

And Raymond Cattell, in his groundbreaking 1954 work on personality factors, identified the traits of a leader as these:

- **Emotional stability:** Good leaders must be able to tolerate frustration and stress. Overall, they must be well adjusted and have the psychological maturity to deal with anything they are required to face.
- **Dominance:** Leaders are often competitive and decisive, and usually enjoy overcoming obstacles. Overall, they are assertive in their thinking style as well as their attitude in dealing with others.
- **Enthusiasm:** Leaders are usually seen as active, expressive, and energetic. They are often very optimistic and open to change. Overall, they are generally quick and alert and tend to be uninhibited.
- **Conscientiousness:** Leaders are often dominated by a sense of duty and tend to be very exacting in character. They usually have a very high standard of excellence and an inward

---

[2] Economy, Peter. "Top 10 Skills Every Great Leader Needs to Succeed." *Inc.* Dec. 29, 2014. www.inc.com/peter-economy/top-10-skills-every-great-leader-needs-to-succeed.html.

desire to do one's best. They also have a need for order and tend to be very self-disciplined.

- **Social boldness:** Leaders tend to be spontaneous risk-takers. They are usually socially aggressive and generally thick-skinned. Overall, they are responsive to others and tend to be high in emotional stamina.

- **Tough-mindedness:** Good leaders are practical, logical, and to the point. They tend to be low in sentimental attachments and comfortable with criticism. They are usually insensitive to hardship and are very poised.

- **Self-assurance:** Self-confidence and resiliency are common traits among leaders. They tend to be free of guilt and have little or no need for approval. They are generally secure and free from guilt and are usually unaffected by prior mistakes or failures.

- **Compulsiveness:** Leaders were found to be controlled and very precise in their social interactions. Overall, they were very protective of their integrity and reputation and consequently tended to be socially aware and careful, abundant in foresight, and very careful when making decisions or determining specific actions.[3]

An important question that has been researched for decades is, "Are leaders born or made?" While I do not have a definitive answer to this, I will attempt to describe within these pages my personal journey to leadership and the lessons I have learned along the way.

---

[3] Quoted in U.S. Small Business Administration. "Leadership Traits." May 16, 2008. https://bit.ly/2VbCkPE.

Chapter 1

The Journey Begins

EARLY YEARS

I was the second of my parents' three daughters, born in Cleveland, Ohio, in the late 1950s. Being the middle child is often problematic because we middle children don't have a distinct role like that of the oldest child or the baby of the family. So we sometimes struggle with what part we play in the hierarchy. This dilemma was solved for me when I heard my mother introduce my sisters and me to someone with the words, "This is my oldest, this is my youngest, and this is the smart one!" Finally, I knew my place in the family! As a result of those words, my self-identity became intimately tied to fulfilling the role my mother ascribed to me.

In elementary school, I strived for all As in my classes—Bs were unacceptable to the point that if I received one, I cried! (Grades of C or below were unheard of.) My mother had no idea why I cried over grades because she didn't know that as the "smart one," I had decided that I had to live up to the title or lose my place in our family.

This extended to keeping up my teachers' beliefs in me. I was blessed with teachers who saw something in me academically and refused to allow me to do less than my best. I often succeeded because of wanting to prove them right in their assessments; they believed in me when I couldn't or didn't believe in myself. So I worked hard to ensure that I lived up to their expectations or their expectations of me were my expectations of myself.

Simultaneously, my home life was chaotic. I never knew when my father would return from a night of drinking with his friends or a weekend with his girlfriend and her children and physically attack my mother.[4] I recall my parents' arguments that became physical, and my sisters and I jumped on my father's back and held his legs to stop him from hitting her. That nightmare lasted until my mother divorced my father when I was seven or eight years old. Unfortunately, the divorce made our two-income household a one-income household. My mom struggled to keep us fed and clothed while my father, who could afford a lawyer when my mom couldn't, traveled the country with his friends and refused to pay his court-ordered child support.

To keep a roof over our heads, my mother decided to marry a man who promised to take care of all of us. So at the age of ten or eleven, I inherited an alcoholic stepfather. I didn't fully understand at the time how dramatically our lives would change, especially due to the embarrassment of having him stagger down the street looking for alcohol or keep us up at night while he attempted to cook and almost burned down the house because he forgot the flame was on. These experiences and others strengthened my commitment to earning a college degree to ensure that my then reality did not become my future reality.

During this period, my identity as the "smart one" became more important to me because it made me study harder to get out of this situation. My mother always stressed the importance of school because her father, who owned a trucking firm in Pittsburgh in the 1950s and 1960s, didn't support her aspiration of becoming a nurse—he didn't think his daughters were worth such an investment. Even though she couldn't pursue her own dream, especially after the divorce with three children under the age of twelve, my mother encouraged my sisters and me to do well and to pursue our goals.

---

[4] There is help. If you are in danger, contact 911, your local domestic abuse organization, the National Domestic Violence Hotline at 1-800-799-7233, or the National Resource Center on Domestic Violence at www.nrcdv.org.

My mom also inspired my dream of becoming a cardiothoracic surgeon. Rather than pursuing nursing, she earned her certification as a surgical technician assisting doctors in the operating room. Her favorite cases involved heart surgery. Her fascination became my career goal and blended well with my desire to earn good grades as the smart child in the family.

Two individuals were instrumental in my academic success in elementary and middle school: Mrs. Mattie Stephens and Dr. Bert Holt. Both had tremendously high expectations of their students. They refused to allow me to give less than my best effort; they taught me that hard work would be worth the sacrifice.

During these years, I began dating a friend of my sister's boyfriend named Jack, who was six years my senior—I was just fourteen and he was twenty. (I lied and told my mom that he was three years older. She believed me because his face looked younger.) Jack was kind and made me feel special, which was a welcome change from feeling that I had to prove myself worthy of anyone's consideration, especially my father's and occasionally my mom's. My boyfriend also had a job and a car—a major accomplishment for a fourteen-year-old young woman! It didn't occur to me until much later that a twenty-year-old shouldn't date a fourteen-year-old because, at the time, I was proud of having a much older boyfriend who could pick me up from school and buy me nice things. What a rush!

Jack was very attentive during our first year of dating. He dropped me off at school, picked me up, purchased my clothes, and even provided me with food. Over time, he eventually became my primary source for everything important to me. He systematically moved me away from my family and friends by occupying most of my time away from school; I could barely breathe but viewed it as positive because he wanted to take care of me.

It took about one year for him—with my unconscious permission—to totally isolate me from my family. That's when the physical abuse began.

I suffered in the relationship for almost five years—ages fourteen to nineteen. As any person who has experienced prolonged abuse will relate, we stay with the abuser because we lived in an abusive environment during our childhood and unconsciously adopted abuse as our norm. The abuser often demonstrates extreme remorse and asks for another chance, which we grant because the abuser shows us flashes of thoughtfulness when not being abusive. In addition, our self-esteem was already compromised before we entered the relationship, so we don't believe we deserve better.

I was ashamed and embarrassed at the time because of how I allowed Jack to treat me. I did reach out to adults for help but with limited success because I didn't want to escape the situation; I simply wanted them to get him to stop hurting me.

The drive to break off the relationship came because of two simple words my abuser shouted: "You're stupid!" This, of course, couldn't be true because I was the smart one in my family, so my personal identity conflicted with the identity Jack wanted to ascribe to me. In addition, I had worked diligently for years to earn grades that would enable me to attend college to pursue my dream of becoming a cardiothoracic surgeon. This vision kept me focused during the difficult periods. In fact, I went to the library and for hours sat immersed in books that helped me dream beyond my current circumstances. I kept repeating to myself, "This will not be my life when I'm an adult!" and "I won't get stuck here!" So his calling me stupid and then later suggesting that I wait a year to attend college flew in the face of my dream—I was going to college no matter the consequences, even the possibility of death at his hands!

COLLEGE AND BEYOND

Earlier, I talked about the teachers who made me want to do my best and shaped me as a student. While their contributions to my growth were positive, a less pleasant memory, but no less impactful, involved my high school honors math teacher, Mr. Binder, who defined me as deficient. That struck at the heart of my identity as the smart one in my family. To this day, I can recall the pain of his statement, "If you don't know that, you don't belong in this class." Unfortunately for me, his public statement in front of eight of my closest friends (there were only nine of us in the class) caused me deep humiliation. I should have risen to the occasion and proved him wrong, but instead, I packed up my books, moved to the last seat in the row, and stopped listening to him, believing that my silence would make him feel guilty enough to apologize. That never happened. In fact, because I stopped listening, I stopped learning, which ultimately resulted in my receiving Ds in every subsequent math class. The only reason I remained in college-level math was the chairwoman of the math department, Mrs. Lelia McBath, refused to let me take easier classes because she knew of my desire to attend college.

I was recruited to attend Stanford University but was afraid to leave home and my boyfriend for the West Coast, so I decided to apply to a selective university in Cleveland, Case Western Reserve University. Unfortunately, earning As in every class except math eventually led to my rejection by Case, the only college to which I applied.

To add salt to my academic wound, when I told Mr. Binder that I applied to Case, he responded, "Do you really think they will admit you?" He was right; they didn't, primarily due to my math grades.

Mrs. McBath knew that my grades in math did not reflect my ability to do the work, so without my knowledge, she contacted an admissions counselor at the university and urged them to interview me. They did and offered me conditional admission contingent on my successfully earning at least a C in advanced math. That decision changed my life!

When I shared the news with Mr. Binder, he said, "I guess they'll admit anybody!" At that point, his words no longer had the ability to cause me pain. I was on my way to that college I desired to attend and planned to do what I should have done before—show him and myself that I was capable. So, I entered college and, with much tutoring, earned an A in advanced math in my first semester and was fully admitted to the university!

Upon arriving at Case, a predominantly white university, I was struck by the fact that I truly was a minority student! I'm sure you're asking yourself, "How is that possible?" The fact was that my high school was overwhelmingly filled with students who looked and spoke like me. As a result, the issue of what it means to be a minority in an educational setting never came up until I matriculated to college.

I distinctly remember walking into my chemistry class and standing at the top of the auditorium-like room, counting the number of Black students enrolled in a class of over 250. There were eight, including me![5] Talk about a wake-up call! It was really my first experience of having to confront what it meant to be Black and a minority in that setting.

Thankfully, there was a program at the university called Student Support Services—one of the eight outreach and student services programs known as the Federal TRIO Programs, which are designed to identify low-income individuals, first-generation college students, and people with disabilities and assist them to progress through the academic pipeline from middle school to postbaccalaureate programs. The programs provide a safe place for first-generation students and Students of Color—African American, Latino, Native American, Pacific Islander. (Asian students were not considered minority students on the campus due to the significant number of international students, primarily from China.) There, the students could receive help with coursework and advice and advocacy on how to navigate school successfully. Student Support Services was a godsend for me and others like me who had earned our places in the university but were perceived to be only "affirmative action" students, whose only value to the university was the color of our skin and not our ability to compete academically.

The first year of school was very difficult because I was in the process of learning how to be a college student while still in a relationship with my abuser. Fortunately for me, the issue with my

---

[5] At the time of my birth, my sisters and I were technically considered "Colored." We became "Black" in the 1960s. In the '80s, we became "African American."

boyfriend came to a head quickly through an unintended, and at the time unwelcome, intervention by a student affairs staff member with whom I shared my secret of abuse. Unbeknownst to me, she was gossiping about my situation to others. When the news reached me, I felt publicly humiliated, enough so to get out of the relationship even with the threat of a severe beating or death hanging over me. Subsequently, I confronted my boyfriend at my mother's house and told him that I was leaving him. He stared at me for a moment. Then he punched me in the face and ran out.

I wish that had been the end of the story, but I made the mistake of trying to remain friends with him at my mom's suggestion. In hindsight, I think this was based on her decision to remain on friendly terms with my father because of my sisters and me. One day, I was running late to school (I lived at home) and missed my bus. Jack called and asked how things were going. I said that I was running late to school, he offered to drive me, and I accepted his offer.

The drive was uneventful until we arrived on campus. When he parked in front of the building, he switched the conversation and began asking me to take him back. I put my head down, snorted, and said no. He took offense, accused me of laughing at him, and then began to hit me around my face and head. I tried to block his blows and get out of the car as quick as possible, but I fumbled for the handle and eventually jumped out of the car. He sped off and I ran into the building, asked for directions to the restroom, and found that he had broken a blood vessel in my eye and my hair was a mess. I looked in the mirror and said, "Maybe Momma won't make me be his friend anymore!"

After I cleaned my face and combed my hair, I found a pay phone and called my mother at work to tell her of his attack and said, "Now, can I stop being his friend?" I learned later that she contacted Jack and threatened to kill him if he ever hit me. I never heard from him again. I eventually learned almost thirty years later that he died in his fifties. I'm sorry to admit it, but I was relieved because he couldn't hurt anyone else.

My freedom from the relationship enabled me to focus on improving my grades. As I recounted earlier, my plan was to become a surgeon; however, I struggled in the classes required for medical school (for example, biology, chemistry, physics, and calculus). Fortunately, I had to take classes to fulfill the global studies requirement. I chose anthropology.

My first class was with Dr. Charles "Charlie" Callendar, who taught me that every culture, including mine as a Black student, was equally important and valued. Charlie provided an international context for me as a Black person in America; while I was a minority in the United States, my people were not a minority in the world! I fell in love with anthropology and majored in whatever class Charlie taught. However, I didn't give up on becoming a surgeon at that time, so I majored in medical anthropology and minored in natural science just in case.

I struggled initially because I wasn't prepared for the transition to a selective college. I was also unprepared academically; I assumed that an A in my high school would be equivalent to an A in college and that my nonexistent study habits, which had earned me good grades in high school, were sufficient for college … wrong!

Two of my favorite memories, which were hurtful at the time, were due to comments of a professor and a dean. I had earned As in every high school English class I took. I was convinced that, with very little work, I would accomplish the same in college, especially since my English score was the highest on my American College Testing (ACT) entrance exam. So, I was surprised and a little miffed that my first graded paper in English earned a D. I made an appointment with the professor and explained my stellar work in high school and how he must be mistaken. He responded, "That was high school. This is college." My face shattered! What he said was a wake-up call that scared me enough that I eventually earned As in five other English courses.

My second encounter was with my academic dean. Because of the life challenges of my transition to college as well as my personal life, some of which I have shared or will share, my grades in my freshman and sophomore years would not allow me to graduate, let alone enter medical school. After taking time away from college (I "stopped out" three times before I graduated), I returned during one of those periods and met with the advisor. I shared with him my dream of becoming a surgeon. He left his office to retrieve my file. When he returned, he reviewed my transcript, raised his head, and said, "Can I be honest with you?" I said that he could. He responded, "Not with this shit, you don't!" He explained that I had to earn at least a 3.0 grade point average for my remaining time in college and earn no less than a B in every biology, chemistry, physics, and math course from then on. I put my head in my hands, took a deep breath, and decided in that moment that I would do whatever it took to raise my grades, including seeking help from tutors and taking mini-courses like notetaking and time management to enhance my irregular study habits.

I became a model student: I scheduled my entire week and included three hours on Thursday to watch television. I was so focused on getting my work done that I paid no attention to my grades other than tracking how well I was doing in individual classes. As a result, I was stunned to learn that I had made the dean's list with over a 3.5 GPA in some of the most difficult classes the college offered! It was the third time that I embraced the fact that my performance in college was fully contingent on my work ethic: when I made a sincere effort, positive results followed. I learned this with my advanced math class that allowed me to be a fully admitted student; when my English professor enlightened me as to the expectations in college and I rose to the occasion five additional times; and finally, when the dean told me that a 3.0 GPA was necessary to follow my dream, and I attained it and more!

I've mentioned that I experienced a few challenges before, during, and after college. One of the most challenging was my marriage to my college sweetheart, Gene. I met Gene in my freshman year; he was one of the handsomest Black students at the college. I fell in lust quickly! However, I was still in the relationship with Jack, but knew

I would be leaving it at some point, so I found ways to hang around Gene in the interim.

In my sophomore year, Gene and I became a couple and began talking about marriage, or more accurately, I began talking about marriage. My desire to marry was twofold: (1) I was trying to be a "good" Christian by adhering to the Bible verse that says, "It is better to marry than to burn" (1 Corinthians 7:9) and (2) I wanted to prove to myself and show my parents that I could marry well and for a lifetime. That didn't happen! Within six months of the wedding, I was miserable; I had to leave college because my marriage made me ineligible to receive grants, only loans that I had no idea how I would pay for after school. (I came from a family that was barely scraping by when my parents divorced ... loans were not an option.) This was devastating to me because my life goals depended on my graduating from college.

My misery turned into deep depression when I also learned that I was pregnant at the exact moment I was losing my child in miscarriage. I felt beyond hopeless, so much so that I began to think of ways to commit suicide.[6]

For two weeks, I could not sleep or eat; I felt like I was living a nightmare! Every thought circled back to my "failures" of being in a terrible marriage after leaving an abusive relationship; having to leave college (my means to a better life) because my marriage made me ineligible for grants; and not being able to bring a child into the world. It hurt to think and to live! So, one day as I wandered around campus, it occurred to me that I could simply walk in front of a bus and people would think it was an accident. I looked to my left and noticed a bus was driving toward me. I closed my eyes and prepared myself to step off the curb, but I suddenly heard my mother's voice tell me that if I killed myself, I couldn't go to heaven. It also flashed through my mind that if I killed myself, with my luck, things would get better but I wouldn't be around to see. With both those thoughts

---

[6] Contemplating suicide is a serious step. If you or someone you know needs assistance, please contact 911, your local suicide prevention organization, or the National Suicide Prevention Lifeline at 1-800-273-8255 or https://suicidepreventionlifeline.org.

rolling around in my head, I stepped away from the curb and walked back to my dorm. (I was able to return to school for a short time after my husband and I separated.)

I don't recall all the details, but once I arrived at the dorm, I told one of my roommates that I planned to kill myself and that I needed to figure out a way so God wouldn't know I was trying to commit suicide. My roommate convinced me to go to counseling and immediately walked with me to the counselors' office. God, through my roommate and my counselor, saved my life! Bettina Katz, the counselor, had me sign a contract that if I felt like harming myself or someone else, I was to contact her. And, since the end of the semester was nearing, I was withdrawn from most of my classes and only kept those I had the energy to complete. My job for the remainder was to focus on my mental health. Each day was the same: I woke up; went to the dining hall to eat; went back to my dorm to study, watch TV, or sleep; and then dressed for my daily counseling sessions.

I've often described my mental breakdown as stuffing my thoughts and feelings in a drawer because I didn't want to deal with them, and the drawer became too full and burst open—kind of like the story of Humpty-Dumpty falling off the wall and not being able to be put together again. But in my case, counseling and some difficult soul-searching and decision making about what I wanted my life to be allowed me to slowly recapture pieces of myself that I allowed to be scattered for too long.

The next eight years brought their share of challenges, including having to leave college three times and go to work for lack of funds and a failed marriage. However, I persisted and graduated with a BA in medical anthropology. These undergraduate experiences helped me to better understand and, as much as I allowed myself, to determine my identity as a Black female first-generation college student—its limitations and opportunities. They also helped me confront several very challenging life experiences—and two life-threatening ones—and recognize that I had to have a bigger vision for my life that was worth sacrificing for, even against people who would try to prevent me from reaching my goals because of their selfishness.

In hindsight, I think that my interest in leadership began with my realization that I had to be my own leader—I had to consciously decide daily that the vision I had for my life was worthy because it was what I wanted, not what someone wanted for me. It also made me fully appreciate that I had the right to determine what or who I considered worth my time and attention after years of bouncing from one experience or relationship to another. With this realization and an ever-growing belief that I was destined for a life much larger than I had lived to that point and that I would eventually have to explain the lessons I learned to others, I became a conscious notetaker on my road to leadership.

Chapter 2

Becoming a Conscious Observer (Notetaking 101)

I recall the period when my interest in becoming someone different—personally and professionally—on the road to a hoped-for future was seeded during my time as an undergraduate recruiter and later an undergraduate academic advisor at Case Western Reserve University. I accepted the position because I believed that my struggles at Case could be helpful to students like me who had no experience with college.

Recruitment of first-generation students, and especially Students of Color, is time intensive primarily because the students and the families often don't have a frame of reference for what is expected of them in the recruitment process. Consequently, recruiters must provide additional support, including establishing trust with the students as well as their parents, before the families believe that the recruiters have honorable intentions and want to see the students succeed. Because of the efforts required to recruit these students, I became invested in their not only attending my university but also earning their degree, which was not what the university paid me to do at that time—my job was to recruit students, period.

What I didn't foresee but should have, considering my college experience, was that many of the first-generation students I recruited unfortunately did not stay, primarily because they could not adjust to life at the university. This didn't sit well with me, so even though my job as recruiter was completed because the students had enrolled, I couldn't abandon my students to the whims of the university. I became their advocate and mentor, which created some discord among my colleagues because I now had two allegiances—one to the new class I was paid to recruit and one to those I had already recruited. This dual focus eventually led to my being approached by the dean of the minority student programs to work for her to create a retention program.

To my surprise, I developed a knack for predicting which students would likely complete their college degrees. What I observed was that these freshmen often talked about themselves in the third person, as if they were actors playing a part. I also observed that their language changed as they learned more of the terminology regularly spoken on college campuses, such as *drop/add*, *pass/fail*, or any number of other terms that were required to navigate the college experience. Further, they changed their clothing to look more like college students than high school ones, and they often paired off with other students or quickly joined an on-campus group to connect themselves more solidly to the college as they found their footing in the new environment.

As a result of my observations, my research interest eventually centered on how a freshman successfully transitions from a culturally constructed high school identity to a college identity and what steps are involved in the process. That led me to hypothesize the process of transition to any role requires a change in self-identity, as demonstrated by my students, that is consistent with the cultural norms and expectations of that new role. Consequently, I realized that my forty-year journey to and success in leadership roles involved lessons I learned including the unconscious and conscious cultural components associated with adapting to a new role. I hope my lessons will be helpful to anyone who chooses the mantle of leadership.

However, before I describe the lessons, I would like to introduce to you the levels of leadership and the mental shifts that I experienced in my journey to the position of CEO.

Chapter 3

Levels of Leadership

The following figure illustrates six levels of leadership based on roles in the corporate structure. Each level requires a perspective and skill set not necessarily required at the previous level, as well as a broadening awareness of one's role and responsibilities within the organization. This is another way of saying that each time a person progresses from one leadership role to another, they must understand the context in which they operate in a different way.

Let me state unequivocally that not everyone should take a leadership position; you should know better than anyone else whether you can face up to the responsibilities and their associated stress. However, if, like me, you feel a pull upward, then be prepared for the ride!

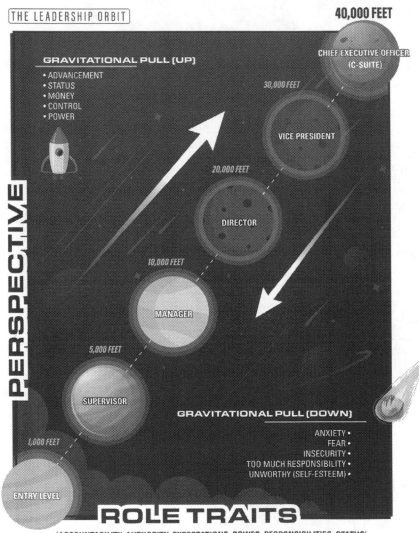

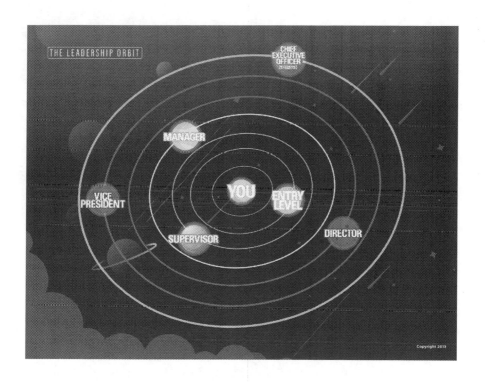

Entry-Level Leader (1,000 Feet)

I began my leadership career in an entry-level position (admissions counselor at a university), in which I was considered management but did not have anyone reporting to me. I was required to work specifically on the program components for which I had responsibility. My view of the larger initiative was limited in scope and did not afford me a broader view of how my contribution affected the entire enterprise.

The perspective at this level required me to spend a great deal of time understanding my role and responsibilities within my department and making sure that I met the goals assigned to me. For example, one of my duties was recruiting high school seniors. I had a specific territory for which I was responsible and a numerical goal for students to matriculate to the university. Most, if not all, conversations with my supervisor focused on my meeting my assigned goals; only rarely did our discussions include the broader recruitment goals of the department. As a result, my perspective was primarily limited to my assignment.

This is what I call the *1,000-foot leadership perspective*.

Supervisor (5,000 Feet)

After several years in two different entry-level leadership positions, I felt the need to pursue a position at the next level at the same university, one that included supervisory responsibility for a small staff. The need arose from my feelings of wanting to contribute on a broader level (that is, have greater influence) and to have more autonomy. I now had a growing family and was also extremely interested in earning more money.

The major difference in the new job was that I now had responsibility for both my own performance and my team's. Unlike in my entry-level leadership positions, as supervisor, I required a broader understanding of the goals of my department and of the division in which the department resided. I also required an understanding of each of my direct reports—their strengths, their weaknesses, and how they worked best, individually and collectively.

In addition to departmental and divisional goals, I had a prescribed set of instructions or rules with which to manage my staff. These were communicated to me by the human resources department. This level afforded me my first opportunity to manage a budget, an important skill for any leader that becomes more so the higher you rise.

While I had more authority in this job than an entry-level leader, my authority was still limited by the department's position within the division, and the division's position within the university.

The supervisor functions at the 5,000-foot leadership perspective.

Manager (10,000 Feet)

When I reached the manager stage, I was often responsible for a project requiring that someone be assigned to complete it—with or without additional staff. I was privileged to experience this twice within the university. The first time, I was tasked with creating a summer program for incoming first-generation college students. While I did not have a staff that reported to me, I was expected to develop a program that interfaced with several administrative and academic departments, the goal of which was to better prepare students for what they would likely encounter in college.

As the manager and developer, I primarily functioned as a facilitator between the students and the various departments to ensure they received the skills necessary to succeed in college. The second project was a new department that interfaced with other departments, with key stakeholders in the neighborhoods that surrounded the university, and with the nonprofit and civic communities. The university had been in the same location for over one hundred years. This new department was created out of the need to establish more productive relationships with the broader community in order to begin a multimillion-dollar construction project, one that required the goodwill and support of affected residents, other community organizations, and city, state and federal officials.

In both these roles, I had to manage my supervisors' and my own expectations of my staff and myself, and establish productive relationships with people at the university and in the community who were important to reaching the goals assigned to my department. My perspective broadened to include an understanding of the roles and responsibilities of other key departments and people necessary to accomplish my departmental goals. At this level, it was incumbent upon me to identify what each stakeholder had to receive in order to actively participate. Another way of saying this is that I had to understand what each person had to get out of their participation in order to feel good about engaging in the program or project. The "What's in it for me?" question is often asked by current and potential participants and must be considered by the manager to be most effective in the role. To adequately answer that question, a 10,000-foot leadership perspective is required.

DIRECTOR (20,000 FEET)

When the university promoted me to director, I viewed it as an acknowledgment by upper management that I could be trusted with a particular department or specific line of business. I felt that I had arrived on the first rung of upper management. At this level, I had authority over a larger staff that included managers or supervisors. I was tasked with creating a Center of Excellence within the university. This was to focus on developing a broader and more cohesive community partnership plan that would involve the entire campus—its operational and academic units.

The title of director within that structure conferred more authority than my previous positions. This made it easier to have discussions with senior-level staff that could result in significant changes to our internal policies and activities in relation to the community. In addition, I was invited to participate in higher-level internal discussions and to serve on committees in other schools and departments, as well as represent the university to the community in a more meaningful way. In other words, at this level, I had more authority to effect change in how my employer conducted its business with the community. But to be effective, I had to broaden my perspective to encompass my boss's expectations and also those of the schools and departments with which I needed to interact in order to meet the goals established for the Center of Excellence.

To function optimally at this level, I had to acquire a 20,000-foot perspective that considered (1) the university's goals for developing the Center, (2) the experiences and perspectives of key community stakeholders relative to the university, (3) the connections within and between schools and departments and their interactions with the community, and (4) what each university and community group identified as their reasons and needs for connecting with each other.

VICE PRESIDENT (30,000 FEET)

My arrival at the vice president level signified my membership on the senior leadership team. I had moved on at this point from the university to a world-renowned cultural museum, the Rock and Roll Hall of Fame. In my new role, I helped the CEO implement his vision in a very formal way. I was also privy to high-level information that directors and managers were not. It was a very heady experience! I felt that I was in rarified air—at this level, staff used to quietly breathe my name and title when mentioning me to new employees. It was amazing! It felt very cliquey in that certain seating areas were reserved just for senior staff at events (always the best tables) and meetings (front and center seats), and for important visitors whenever they came to town.

At this level, I was responsible for a division (rather than a department) within my organization. I reported directly to the CEO and engaged in high-level planning for the organization.

I also attended board of directors meetings and represented my employer to the community. The title of vice president conferred upon me a significant amount of authority within and outside of the organization. When I spoke on its behalf, I represented my supervisor, the CEO; I had his imprimatur and was certain that my words had weight as a result.

To be effective at this level, I had to adopt a 30,000-foot view. This required a broadening of my perspective—it had to be organizational, with a keen understanding of how my division must be structured to meet the goals for not only my division but also the institution.

Like an orchestra musician whose conductor was the CEO, I had to understand all the parts of the music to play my part well: I saw my division as the string section, which had to play the appropriate notes at the appropriate time while listening to the other instruments. I was always mindful to work collaboratively with the other vice presidents and their teams. This ensured the organization's success and acknowledgment for my team's efforts in accomplishing its goals.

CHIEF EXECUTIVE OFFICER (40,000 FEET)

The chief executive officer or CEO (also called the *president*) is the highest-level official in an organization. I reached this level after twenty years of working in nonprofits.

To be honest, I was not sure if I wanted to be a CEO because of the significant responsibilities, especially having worked with or reported to people in this position for much of my career. However, the CEO can also effect change in the organization just by virtue of the role and the authority and power ascribed to it.

I distinctly recall the day that changed my mind about being a CEO. There was a tricky situation in which my boss involved me that—even as a vice president—I had limited authority to handle. That day, I said, "If I have to take this grief, I may as well be running the show!" Thereafter, I began looking for opportunities to lead a nonprofit.

My first CEO position was heading a start-up music museum slated for Atlanta, Georgia. I was the house cleaner, cook, and bottle washer, so to speak, in that I was responsible for developing the entire organization, including writing the business plan, recruiting board members and staff, and finding funding to support the initiative. While I was successful in achieving the majority of my goals, I was unable to raise enough money. There was competition nearby in the form of a similar museum that was much further along in the planning process. As a result, the organization folded—but not without giving me some important lessons that were absolutely vital for my next CEO position.

My second chance at CEO came one year later, after I returned to my hometown of Cleveland, Ohio. My predecessor, "Ms. Townsend," had recently been convicted of a felony, and the organization experienced tremendous upheaval as a result.

My initial response to an inquiry by an executive headhunter was a categorical no because I did not want the headache that would be associated with an organization in crisis, even though I knew myself to be a change agent who thrives in sometimes difficult or challenging environments. What eventually made me decide to enter the applicant pool were the mission of the organization and the pull to this leadership position that, I believed, God gave me. Over one hundred people applied, and I was selected!

I cannot fully describe the chaos that existed when I arrived and the chaos that happened shortly afterward at all levels of the organization, including the board. In fact, one of my colleagues and I said that if anyone asked us to write a book about our experience, the title would be *You Can't Make This S**t Up!* Every aspect of the organization had to be assessed, eliminated, or updated because they were all antiquated, nonfunctional, or dysfunctional. I often described it as a $40 million mom-and-pop store because most of the systems were either manual or based on old policies or understandings of old policies. In many cases, procedures were performed automatically, without any regard for efficiency or effectiveness. However, even with the chaos, the staff served our clients well.

My charge was to create a new vision for the organization, primarily by reminding everyone of our mission—our *why* for existing. I also had to change the culture from one of silos and box checking to a collaborative learning culture. This necessitated developing a team of seasoned professionals who shared my mindset and vision and creating enough positive momentum to overwhelm the naysayers.

As I write this, I have just begun my sixth year as CEO. And while we have accomplished an enormous amount, especially in terms of change in the organizational culture and the infrastructure that supports that change, we have much more to do.

To function optimally at this level, I had to adopt a 40,000-foot perspective that includes the following.

- I understand the role of the board of directors as a whole and each director's thoughts as they relate to the organization (that is, its mission and how to achieve it).
- Rather than being part of the orchestra, as I described at the previous level, I am now the conductor: I do not need deep knowledge of how to play the instruments; that is the responsibility of the staff and the leadership team. I am instead responsible and accountable for the entire musical score— every note each instruments plays and when. As CEO, I cannot know the intricacies of each part of the organization. But a breadth of knowledge of the entire organization and specific mastery of key metrics, especially the finances and those associated with each area, are required.
- Recognizing that my words have power internally and externally, I need to be mindful of what, how, and to whom I speak.
- I acknowledge that my presence or lack thereof confers a particular meaning to employees. My "showing up" at events or visiting our various offices demonstrates to staff that I care

about them, but only if I demonstrate that my motive is being accessible and concerned about their well-being, not checking to see if they are working. (I have come to understand that, because of my job title, my presence changes the atmosphere in the room; for example, people are less willing to share their thoughts if I attend a meeting.)

- I realize that I do not have the luxury of acting afraid or uncertain before my staff. They want to feel secure in the knowledge that, like a captain of a ship, I as the CEO am steady at the wheel, directing the ship's course.

- I recognize that I am always a role model, in all places. As such, I must be careful about how I treat people, in addition to how I communicate with them. In other words, I must model the behavior I would like staff to emulate. This includes apologizing when I make mistakes and doing what's right even when no one is looking.

- I had to become consciously aware that, like Atlas, I hold up the entire organization—it will rise or fall based on my leadership. Knowing and owning this is a privilege and humbling, but also—because our staff's livelihoods depend on it—incredibly stressful.

My journey through these levels of leadership provided me important lessons that I continue to draw on today. The following twenty-six lessons were gained over forty years through trial and error, tribulation and success, and an overwhelming commitment to being and becoming an effective and compassionate servant leader and helping others do the same.

Chapter 4

Lessons in Leadership

LESSON #1: WHAT DO I SEE?
A LEADERSHIP PERSPECTIVE

I can't say that one day I simply decided to assume or pursue a leadership role. In fact, I had always defined myself as a really good support person—someone who didn't need the limelight and was very content to contribute behind the scenes. However, I noticed that people kept moving me from the shadows to the forefront. I was extremely uncomfortable at first but eventually realized others saw leadership skills in me that I didn't see in myself, and I needed to make a decision: Would I remain in my comfort zone in the supporting positions I saw myself as deserving, or step forward and assume a larger role based on what others believed to be true of me? This was a major turning point in my life and my career. In fact, it felt like I was looking down into an abyss, trying to decide if the jump from the familiar was worth the effort or would result in my possible (career) death.

I discussed the matter with a trusted advisor, who happened to be at the same crossroad. We both decided that we had to take the risk because we wanted our jobs to have a greater effect on our community. So, taking my courage and leaning on my faith, I jumped into the unknown.

The Bible states it this way:

> Ye are the light of the world. A city that is set on an hill cannot be hid.
>
> Neither do men light a candle, and put it under a bushel, but on a candlestick; and it giveth light unto all that are in the house.
>
> Let your light so shine before men, that they may see your good works, and glorify your Father which is in heaven. (Matthew 5:14–16)

People who pursue leadership roles often must make a conscious decision to go higher in their current organization or move upward in a different organization. I have equated the "pull of leadership" with the gravitational pull a planet operates within to remain in its orbit; each leadership level has an orbit in which the individual operates. The orbit comprises what I term *role traits*: one's accountability, authority, expectations, power, responsibilities, and status.

The gravitational pull upward may be influenced by rewards such as money, status, control, power, and authority. However, as Sir Isaac Newton postulated in his third law of physics, "For every action, there is an equal and opposite reaction." This is also true for the pull to leadership. Forces such as anxiety, fear of the unknown, insecurity, dislike of responsibility, and self-esteem problems (a feeling of unworthiness) may either prevent an individual from pursuing the next level or cause the individual to fail. Unless people recognize the pull downward as part of the process of entering a higher orbit, they may choose to remain where they are because it is too great a risk to leave what they know for something unknown that will invariably have more responsibility and more opportunities to fail on a grander scale.

People who are prepared move upward with the knowledge that the next level of leadership will have its own challenges that, given their history of success, they will be able to handle. Additionally, while these people may be cognizant of the potential to fail, they focus their attention instead on the positive impact they believe they can make at the next level.

Lesson #2: Reasons to Lead—Passion, Desire, and Wanting to Make a Difference

As far back as I can remember, I have wanted to contribute in some way—to a project, to a cause, or to making something or someone better. It is my passion! To me, leadership without passion for the work is just a job; I get paid to do it whether I care about it or not. I have had a few jobs that did not require passion; they required that I show up each day, put in my requisite hours, and perform adequately. However, after experiencing enough of those, I decided that I would shift my thinking from what the job entailed to how well I performed it. I adopted the motto, "I never want to be the weak link on any team." Consequently, my passion and heartfelt desire became meeting my high personal standards of performance in whatever position I held.

Over time, I began to include as part of my search criteria a passion for the mission of the organization and the work for which I would be responsible. I have found that I perform better in an environment or role when my passion is present; passion allows me to contribute at a deeper level.

For example, I found myself in a role that I was initially enthusiastic about and salivated over because of the job description's stated expectation regarding the difference the university could make and because of my interview to connect the university to my community in more meaningful ways. As a native Clevelander, this was music to my ears and one of my heartfelt desires. Unfortunately, I learned that the real intent was to co-opt the community to move the university's agenda rather than create real relationships with its neighbors (the university is an urban campus surrounded by neighborhoods). I came to this realization slowly because many of the ideas I had, which I shared during my initial interview for the position, were summarily dismissed or watered down.

After about a year in the job, I asked my supervisor, "Bill," if he was willing to walk with me on campus to have a frank conversation about his and the university's expectations for my job. I asked that he be honest with me—that he tell me if he couldn't respond to a question with a direct answer, rather than hedge. Bill agreed, and we walked and talked for about an hour, after which I understood what I could reasonably accomplish, which in my mind amounted to window dressing—it looks nice on the surface, but it isn't real. That was not what I had agreed to do when I accepted the position. Consequently, my initial passion and desire for the job turned into keen dissatisfaction, and I began looking for another job that I could care deeply about.

On the reverse side, some of my fondest memories are from when I was an academic advisor to Students of Color who, like me, were the firsts in their family to go to college. Each student became my child, and I took a personal interest in their success; my passion was to see them walk across the stage to receive their undergraduate degree. I loved my job because their success was my success! To this day when I see my former students, many of whom have done exceptionally well in life, they hug and thank me for my support, and I glow like a proud mother!

If given the choice between money and passion, desire, and a willingness to make a difference, I will always put money in last place; passion, desire, and a willingness to make a difference are absolutes.

LESSON #3: CHOOSING TO REMAIN BEHIND THE SCENES OR STEPPING FORWARD

I distinctly remember the day that I chose to move from a supporting role to a leadership one. A colleague and I shared similar professional experiences in which others either nominated us for some leadership position or appointed us to lead some project. We were both dismayed because we felt more comfortable behind the scenes instead of up front. He said, "I guess God is trying to tell us something." I agreed, and that day, I shifted my thinking to allow for broader roles than I would have previously entertained.

Not long after our conversation, I found myself in some committee meeting and was adding my thoughts to the discussion. Shortly before a vote was to be taken to determine the committee chair, I excused myself to go to the restroom. When I returned, I was notified that I had been elected to chair the committee. I was floored! I had not sought this position, nor did I want the responsibility, but this clearly demonstrated that my coworkers thought I could handle it.

That experience confirmed what my colleague and I had discussed previously: God said that it was time to step forward. It also helped me decide to never again leave a meeting before all the votes have been taken!

LESSON #4: SOMETIMES OTHERS HAD TO BELIEVE FOR ME

The experience of having other people believe in me when I did not believe in myself has happened too many times in my life, especially in my early years when I was striving to create a situation distinctly different from my dysfunctional life prior to attending college.

I was fortunate to have wonderful mentors, primarily in the form of teachers and administrators who saw something wonderful in me. Because of their beliefs in my abilities, I strove to prove them right even when I was not certain they were. Each one held me to an extremely high standard and would not let me give less than my best.

My elementary school teacher Mattie Stephens came into my life during a stressful time. My parents were going through a divorce. My father often chose to not pay child support, and we had to move to an area that was economically depressed, as indicated by the number of boarded-up or dilapidated homes on my street. The brightest spot in my day was attending school because my teacher took a particular interest in me, kept me near her after school, and assigned me challenging work. She was the first teacher to set the bar higher for me because, as she said, "I know you can do more than you're showing me." So, I did.

My middle school teacher Mrs. Holt, who later became Dr. Holt, believed that each child in her class was capable of greatness. She treated us as brilliant young people who would someday change the world; she introduced that world to us in her classroom and expanded my thinking beyond the street on which I lived. My love of learning about new places and my desire to see the world were formed by her!

As I recounted previously, I had a difficult transition to college due to my insecurities as a first-generation Black college student, and I later learned that my school had provided me with inadequate educational preparation (that is, getting an A in an underfunded inner-city school district does not necessarily translate to being prepared to attend a selective university). After having a little success in college, meaning that I was able to maintain a high-enough grade point average to remain there, I approached my academic advisor about attending medical school, which had been my goal since elementary school. He asked me to wait while he retrieved my file. After his review, he said, "Can I be honest with you?" I said yes, and he proceeded with a very candid discussion of my capabilities that left me in no doubt as to where I stood. He said, "Not with this shit, you don't!" In that moment, I had a decision to make: to either accept his opinion or argue against it. I chose to listen because I believed that he had my best interests in mind and was trying to help me even if his words hurt me.

This is not to say that our meeting was all bad. In fact, he gave me some suggestions as to how I could improve my chances of acceptance to medical school. I am proud to say my grades improved substantially and, even though I later decided not to pursue my dream, that advisor wrote my recommendation to the graduate program from which I later earned my master's degree and PhD in psychological anthropology.

Every promotion was a leap of faith for me. I stepped out in faith remembering the support I have had from informal and formal mentors who believed in me when I was not certain that I could do a job. I'm incredibly thankful for their support through the years, which has enabled me to share these lessons with you.

LESSON #5: MY AUTHORITY VERSUS MY INFLUENCE

In my first few jobs, I believed that *leadership* meant the authority or power to accomplish goals. One of the most profound leadership lessons I have learned since then is the difference between authority and influence.

In one of my previous positions, I complained to my boss that I was frustrated by having little authority. I felt that I could have only a limited effect. This man's influence within the organization was substantially greater than that associated with his formal title. He listened to my tale of frustration, then replied that he felt he was a failure if he had to use his authority to get things done. He believed that a leader's greatest power was the ability to influence people rather than to dictate to them. Realizing that he was correct was an important paradigm shift for me.

Instead of complaining for the rest of my tenure at that organization, I became a student of learning what needs each person in a process had to have fulfilled in order for them to feel good about their participation. I adopted the attitude that I would be an honest broker or a master at facilitating mutually beneficial outcomes. This resulted in my influence growing, as demonstrated by a marked increase in the number of invitations I received to attend meetings or participate in projects that were often outside of my prescribed responsibilities.

LESSON #6: PERSONAL MISSION STATEMENT

I have been fortunate to have wonderful bosses who also pushed me to become better.

One of them asked me a thoughtful question regarding my communication style: "Is your candor intended to intimidate or to inform?" I responded, "It all depends." To this, he suggested that I tell people in advance about my method of communication.

Shortly afterward, I shared this conversation with one of my anthropology professors, who explained the cultural difference in communication between Whites and Blacks. He said that Whites are taught to read between the lines, whereas Blacks are taught to communicate more directly. Consequently, misunderstandings could occur between the two because of their styles of communicating. His explanation helped me to understand my boss's comment and to develop what I have come to call my personal mission statement of "open, honest, direct communication." Now, at the beginning of any new relationship, I share my personal mission statement and ask if the person or persons are comfortable with it. Invariably, everyone with whom I have shared it has answered affirmatively, and this sets the tone for all subsequent discussions.

LESSON #7: STANDING, FALLING, OR LYING DOWN—VALUES AND INTEGRITY

I am fortunate to have had few challenges to my values, but it has been extremely helpful to know what those are or were. I have found that my values became clearer when they were challenged or when I saw people I admired acting in ways that fell short of my expectations.

Years ago, I was asked by an employer to do something that was, if not illegal, borderline unethical. At the risk of losing my job, I told him I should not have been placed in a situation that could have resulted in negative consequences for either of us. On another occasion, my boss, who had been a major, influential figure within the organization, was relegated to a lower position of influence; while his title did not change, his access to the CEO did. This resulted in a significant shift in his behavior and caused him to operate with less transparency and, in my opinion at the time, less integrity. From these experiences, I adopted the philosophy that you cannot predict what a person will do in a high-pressure situation, so do not be surprised when someone you admire acts carelessly when stressed.

My greatest challenge so far has been as the leader of an organization in crisis. At the time I was hired, my job was to revitalize it. Unfortunately, members of the board of directors had become intimately involved in the day-to-day operations of the organization, which violated the code of regulations or bylaws. This resulted in a power struggle between me as the CEO and them as my supervisors. War was declared on both sides, and it became fodder for the local media. My integrity was questioned, as was my ability to lead the organization.

I remember sitting in my office after the board voted to terminate me, asking God if I had done what was required of me and whether it was time to leave. Surprisingly, this moment of weakness strengthened me. I straightened my back, felt a renewed energy to fight for the organization and my professional reputation, and eventually did both and won. My reputation was restored, my integrity was intact, and by standing up to what I knew to be false claims, I earned the respect of countless leaders who had watched the war at a distance.

Lesson #8: Leadership Means Having a Bull's-Eye on Your Back—The Need for Authenticity and Thick Skin

The preceding board situation I recounted required that I develop "thick skin," meaning the ability to take professional blows without crumbling. I did not always have this ability; it was built over time from some difficult circumstances.

For much of my life, I had a need to be liked and to be well thought of. In fact, for years I have compared myself to a chameleon— whatever color you need me to be, I am happy to oblige if you want me as part of the exchange. I have often joked that I deserve an Academy Award for the times that I played the part of Jacklyn Chisholm—the strong, unshakeable Black heroine.

This persona changed when I moved to Atlanta to lead the museum project, the project did not receive funding, and I subsequently moved back home with my tail tucked between my legs. During this period, everything I thought true of me was thrown into question. In particular, the question that constantly ran through my mind was, *Who am I when I do not have a job title associated with my name?*

Doing the important work of deep personal reflection caused me to rethink how I perceived myself and others, especially the need to be liked rather than respected by my peers. By the time I returned to the workplace, I knew that I had changed—I had made the decision to live authentically and more fearlessly, which, in turn, made me less vulnerable to attacks and second-guessing when someone disagreed with or attacked me. Without having gone through this experience, I am certain that I would not have successfully transitioned to the role of CEO of a multimillion-dollar organization.

LESSON #9: PERMISSION TO ENTER THE LEADERSHIP CLUB

I remember the first time I realized that my leadership position placed me in rarified air, so to speak. I had been promoted to director of a newly created office and suddenly received an invitation to the organization's annual holiday party. Having worked at the organization for several years without receiving an invitation—in fact, I had not known the holiday party existed—I approached my boss about it. He informed me that, as a director, I was eligible to attend.

My initial response was, "How did I not know this existed?" My second response was, "Wow, I'm now a member of the 'club'!" I equate this situation to football, my favorite sport, wherein both coaches and quarterbacks are members of an elite group of athletes: while the players are important, these two positions lead their teams—the coaches determining the plays and the quarterbacks guiding the other players to execute them.

Often, by virtue of a title, I was afforded respect and consideration before I had earned them based on my actions. I have found that, prior to earning the title and becoming a member of the club, I had to be relatively clear about who I was and what I hoped to contribute to the organization in my role.

Leadership is equated with power—prescribed and ascribed—both of which, if not managed well, can cause anyone to forget why they wanted the position in the first place. Lord Acton, an English Catholic historian, is credited with saying, "Power tends to corrupt, and absolute power corrupts absolutely." No truer words have been spoken! Too many wonderful people who seek leadership as a means of making their part of the world better become captivated by the power and forget the responsibility to lead well. Every leader must be mindful and wary of this.

LESSON #10: FEARS AND OTHER GHOSTS AND GOBLINS—IMPOSTOR SYNDROME

My biggest fear as a leader is failing or falling short of what the position requires. In almost every job, I have had to fight the thought that someone is going to pull the cover from me and reveal that I am not up to the task—that I am an impostor pretending to know what I am doing when I do not. I am not sure if every leader has this issue or only those of us who have started far behind in life and find themselves in what I have called *rarified air.*

I've begun looking for the origins of my impostor syndrome in my childhood, as many people who had difficult upbringings experience. I question if any of these experiences created a lack of confidence in me and the need to look outside of myself for validation. I believed that if I "behaved," I could stop the violence that was directed at my mother. I thereby believed that I was responsible for someone else's actions—that, somehow, I caused the attacks because of my behavior. I believed that I needed to prove my worth as the "smart one" in my family, so my grades and others' opinions took precedence over me. I believed that it was necessary to pretend to the world that all was well at home when it wasn't. I believed that my father's neglect, rejection, and abandonment of my sisters and me was due in part to our not being important enough to him. (His friends and mistresses took precedence.) I believed that I thought I was better than friends in school and family members later because of their comments about my grades and college. So I downplayed my accomplishments and stopped talking about how my world opened up because of college, et cetera.

Infinite experiences caused me to perform the role of Jackie in the story of Jacklyn Alice Johnson Chisholm and led to my feeling like, any minute, someone would realize that I wasn't as good as I said I was or they thought me to be. In hindsight, I deserve an Oscar for my performance as the lead actress in my own drama! I'm thankful that, even though I still have thoughts of inadequacy run through my mind (*Can I really do this job? What if someone finds out that I'm not as confident as I appear? What if my decisions jeopardize my staff or the organization?*) and I feel paralyzed by them, I can choose how I respond by tapping into memories of past and current successes to remind me that the fears are groundless. It may take seconds or minutes before I am able to come out of the fog, shake it off, and move forward.

Lesson #11: Personal and Professional Scripts—My Constructed Narrative

I have been telling myself and other people stories about me my entire life. Each one has built on the previous ones or, in some cases, overwritten them. This was especially true as I learned more about myself through positive and negative experiences that shaped my identity.

My current narrative reads as follows: I, Jacklyn Chisholm, am a first-generation college graduate, a Black female who, through hard work, persistence, and faith, earned three degrees, including a doctorate. I grew up in an inner city in Ohio. I was predominantly raised by a single parent in a dysfunctional household. I was labeled the "smart" and responsible middle child of three, who was expected to do well in life by her parents, teachers, and key supporters. I can be described as ambitious, principled, a little anal-retentive, and very goal oriented. I overcame personal challenges, including domestic abuse and thoughts of suicide, to have a successful thirty-five-year marriage, two phenomenal children, and two amazing grandchildren. I am a person who values directness and seeks to be empathetic and compassionate; who wants to make whatever she chooses to engage in better because of her participation; who enjoys bringing order to chaos, being an honest broker, and creating mutually beneficial partnerships and results; and who wants to inspire others to pursue their dreams and to help them along their journeys.

It has taken my lifetime to crystallize this narrative. It guides my decision making. It is my north star. It keeps me grounded.

There is a danger in having a personal or professional narrative that is untrue because, eventually, the truth will come to light. So, I have committed myself to telling my truth as I know it, and to being completely authentic in my interactions with people. That way, I do not have to remember who I need to be in a certain situation. "Dr. Jackie" is more than sufficient!

Lesson #12: Change Agent or Manager—There Is a Difference

I recognized the distinction between change agent and manager late in my career. In fact, I realized it while revising my résumé because of the number of positions or responsibilities that had *first* associated with them: first coordinator of a minority scholars' program, first director of an office of community relations, first vice president of planning and external affairs at a world-renowned music museum, first president (founder) of a consulting company, and first CEO of an attempted museum start-up.

I thrive in environments where I get to create something out of nothing or where total reconstruction is required rather than a simple renovation. Total reconstruction, to use a building analogy, requires tearing down all or a substantial portion of a house and rebuilding it (a change agent), while a simple renovation may simply require updating the house's paint job (a manager).

To use another analogy, firefighters (change agents) run to a fire while everyone else is running away from it. I am that firefighter; if something has never been done before, you want me at the table. Once I understood this, I could share it with anyone who might be considering me for a position. For example, during my interview for my current job, I stated, "I am a change agent. Don't hire me if you don't want things to change; don't waste your time or mine." They hired me anyway!

Change agents have a limited shelf life, meaning that we understand we will not be permanent fixtures in an organization. Our job—to use a third analogy—is to right the ship and correct her course. Once this is completed, we move on to the next challenge because to stay would not only diminish our value to the organization but also increase our boredom with the enterprise.

Lesson #13: Leading in Chaos and Transition

Change agents, also called *transitional leaders*, are often hired to bring order to chaos or to reinvent or resurrect an organization in need of help. Six years ago, the nonprofit I currently have the privilege of leading was in the middle of a crisis: its former CEO had been convicted of a felony and was jailed. The organization was the focus of negative publicity that resulted in funders and other key stakeholders questioning its continued viability. My role was to renew faith in the organization and to reestablish it as a necessary and important community asset.

My first step was to acknowledge the difficulties, set a vision for the organization, and establish ground rules going forward. This included the values I hoped to reinforce as we sought to change the organization's culture. I gave our staff a written explanation of our mission (who we are and why we exist) and of how we serve, and I ensured they understood that we are each accountable for our behavior and that making mistakes is okay—fixing them gives us a chance to learn and grow in the process. In condensed form, these ground rules became our "council code," which reads:

To provide excellent service to our customers, we will:

- Put forth our best effort every day;
- Raise significantly our level of expectations;
- Treat one another with respect;
- Try new approaches;
- Apologize and learn from mistakes;
- And be ambassadors in the community

Because we transform lives.

My next challenge was to decide on my leadership team members based on their backgrounds and mindsets. I determined that, of my eight direct reports—all vice presidents—just one was consistent with my goals for the organization. A mentor had counseled me that "a new broom sweeps clean, but slowly." Instead of firing staff members whom I no longer wanted on my leadership team, I changed their titles and moved them one step down in the organization but did not reduce their salaries. Instead, I gave them an opportunity to prove their value to me and the goals I had set for the organization. I then identified external candidates, who had the attitude and experience I believed necessary to move the organization forward, to take their places. I was also very aware that, given the negative publicity, I had to hire people who were known commodities within the community and had strong reputations as professionals. Hiring them indicated that I was building a credible and respected team who would oversee the organization's renaissance.

Because it had been reported to me that the previous administration led by intimidation and bullying, I made a concerted effort to manage by walking around. I visited every site and committed to interviewing all 423 employees to learn about each and to give them an opportunity to hear my vision and to ask me questions one-on-one. This single activity helped catalyze the cultural change I was endeavoring to make. It also helped me to better understand the organization from multiple perspectives and identify issues that needed to be addressed, especially compensation and communication.

Simultaneously, I began a review of our internal processes with the help of several consultants in human resources, finance, information technology, and, especially, board governance, which had become problematic because of the board of directors' previous inappropriate involvement in day-to-day operations. These external reviews, along with the staff interviews, helped me develop a template for the organization.

What became glaringly apparent from these interviews was that the organization was fractured; instead of using an integrated approach to execute its mission, it had been identifying and ranking the systems, processes, and staff according to which financial grant supported them. For example, one government grant accounted for 77 percent of the organization's budget. Consequently, the staff members paid from that fund were perceived to be more important and the remaining staff less so. To address this perceived disparity,

I consistently communicated the value of each member of the staff. No role, including mine, was more important than any other; each had value to carrying out the organization's mission.

I also implemented a policy of telling staff the truth as I understood it in response to their questions. Unfortunately, the previous administration, according to employees, had promoted the concept of "do as I say, not as I do," which is inherently hypocritical. One vice president had also shared with a community partner, "People try to give me their ideas; I tell them what to think." You can imagine that, with this kind of culture reinforced daily, employees were afraid to voice concerns or to express ideas or opinions. So, my leadership team and I gave staff permission to share their perspectives and to offer suggestions to improve our programs, services, and internal operations.

We have begun our sixth year of organizational cultural change. Much has improved in that time. Staff no longer anonymously complain to our funding sources that they have no voice within the organization. We have implemented fair and equitable merit-based performance evaluations and salary increases, which had previously been a major source of discontent because of the previous administration's seeming cronyism. I remain encouraged that, eventually, the cultural and systemic changes we have instituted will allow the organization to serve its employees and clients well into the future.

LESSON #14: CASTING VISION AND BRINGING OTHERS ALONG

The CEO or anyone in a leadership position is considered the captain of the ship, so to speak—we set the ship's course, assign tasks to the crew members, and manage their performance, all with an eye toward reaching the destination.

I have been privileged to work for many wonderful supervisors who not only were clear in their expectations of me and my assignments but also recognized the freedom I needed to perform at my highest level. In other words, they gave me room to spread my wings and understood how high I could fly. In addition, and equally important, they shared their vision with me, which enabled me to understand how my contributions fit into reaching the goals they established for the organization.

As mentioned, several of the jobs I held were new; I had the responsibility to determine their shape and structure. This required that I first create a vision for the department that was consistent with the organization's mission and clearly articulate the role I would play in carrying it out. Of particular note is the idea that has been stated this way: "If you don't know where you're going, any road will take you there." My team looks to me as the leader to know where we are headed and to have some plan, even if it must be modified on occasion.

The vision must be aspirational yet doable—it cannot be unattainable. If a critical mass of my staff, especially my leadership team, cannot see the vision and support it, it is doomed to fail. As a result, I have had to make a concerted effort to first understand the organization—its current position within a particular market or community—in order to perceive the gap it could fill if given a new direction or minimally reimagined to increase its relevance to its clients and the community.

LESSON #15: LEARNING THE *WE* IN LEADERSHIP AND THE *I* IN FALLING SHORT

Other leadership books have covered this lesson well, but I feel compelled to include it because it is an important part of leadership: when we do well as an organization, it's *our* doing, but when we fall short, the leader takes—or should take—full responsibility for the failure. This was a hard lesson for me to learn because, while I happily (or out of necessity, depending on the circumstances) own my failures, rarely in my personal life do I take responsibility for someone else's. Then again, I am not often put in situations in my personal life where I must own others' failures. In my business life, this happens more than I would like and more than I expected.

As the CEO of a nonprofit, I am responsible for the entire enterprise—the good and the bad. I am ultimately accountable to the board of directors for everything that happens in our organization. I cannot make excuses when we fall short; I acknowledge the situation, apologize on behalf of the organization and my team, and make the necessary corrections to ensure the problem does not happen again. As I noted previously, these actions are consistent with our council code, which calls for us to "apologize and learn from mistakes."

In cases where a staff member created the situation, I meet privately with the staff member to discuss the specifics of what happened, including the steps that led to the failure or shortfall. If I believe the person should be held accountable because of this decision making's effect on the organization or our clients, key stakeholders, or funders (for example, loss of money or goodwill), I do so through an official verbal or written warning. Termination is only necessary if the actions jeopardized the organization in some way or were illegal or unethical. However, if I consider the situation a teachable moment because the outcome was not that grievous, the employee and I discuss what happened, lessons learned, next steps, and what the employee must do to address and, if possible, resolve the situation.

Lesson #16: Admitting Mistakes without Losing Authority and Credibility

As CEO, I established from the outset that I would make mistakes—we all do. In fact, I acknowledged my humanity as soon as I arrived at the organization. I told our employees that I was not perfect and that I would wake up every morning thinking about them and looking for ways to improve the organization for our staff and our clients. I asked for their help and, more importantly, invested in more than five years and 423 one-on-one meetings to introduce myself to employees. During these meetings, I shared my vision for and perspective about the organization, learned about the employees' reasons for joining the organization and any ideas they had for how we could improve it, and provided them an opportunity to ask me questions.

That multiyear investment and the changes in the organization's policies and processes that resulted from their suggestions generated significant goodwill with employees. Now, when I make a mistake, I apologize without losing authority and credibility, because they each have had a personal experience with me and had a glimpse into who I am and what matters to me.

In each interaction with staff, I remind them of my personal mission statement of "open, honest, direct communication." I have also added a couple of new statements due to the tone some employees used with me in large group settings: (1) "Be careful how you speak to me; ask your questions in a manner that you would want someone to ask you" and (2) "If you ask me a question, be prepared to hear the answer; you may not like the response, but it will be my truth as I understand it today."

I cannot emphasize enough that creating a foundation of honesty and meeting with staff personally has paid significant dividends for the organization and me as the leader.

LESSON #17: SEEKING HELP WHEN NEEDED—THE ATLAS SYNDROME

I learned about Atlas during my study of Greek mythology as a teenager. According to the story, this massive Titan was condemned to hold the "celestial spheres" on his shoulders. Later sculptural renditions showed Atlas holding up the earth. I often describe leadership, especially at the CEO level, in this way. The CEO is responsible for leading the organization, which sometimes feels as though I am holding the entire enterprise on my shoulders.

This was especially true when I joined an organization in transition and the board and staff looked to me as the leader to set things right and to point my metaphorical finger in a direction and say, "We're going that way!" My arrival there was met with hope and excitement as well as alarm: those who wished for new leadership were thrilled, while those who had benefited by the previous administration were wary. At that time, the setbacks caused by the previous administration had adversely affected its credibility with staff and funding agencies. My job as change agent was, and remains, reestablishing its relevance and positive reputation. This required operating transparently, acknowledging and learning from mistakes, and always remaining mindful of the staff members who perform our work and the clients we serve.

Unfortunately, the weight of my responsibilities has resulted in bruxism (that is, tooth-grinding) and the need to use a bite guard. These physical aches and pains, as well as frequent emotional highs and lows—they're all in the service of the organization. Exercise helps, especially when I do it, but over time, I have learned that the challenge of leadership is to hold up the earth while taking care of yourself.

I am still a work in progress in this lesson.

LESSON #18: PEOPLE ARE ALWAYS WATCHING

I attended the Christmas party of a former boss several years ago. I was an up-and-coming executive on a reconnaissance mission with a well-respected woman at the top of her profession. I asked her, "What three things have you learned as CEO?" She replied, "People are always watching, people are always watching, and people are always watching." She told me that she was always conscious of where she was and how she looked because she never knew when she might meet one of her staff outside of work.

I understood the concept at the time and thanked her for the insight. Years later when I became a CEO, her words instantly came to mind when I was in the ladies' room at a pool and one of our employees spoke to me. (I knew she was an employee not because I was personally acquainted with her—we have over 420 employees— but because her use of my title of Dr. Chisholm alerted me to her association with our agency. Prior to becoming CEO, I seldom had my PhD referenced; however, at this organization, everyone is either *Ms.*, *Mr.*, or *Dr.*) On many occasions since then, I have met staff at the grocery store, at a concert, at an amusement park, et cetera. Consequently, I wear makeup and maintain my appearance regardless of where I go because I know unequivocally that "people are always watching."

This is equally true of my role as the representative of my organization: others are watching what I say, how I say it, and how I conduct myself. I have learned to communicate succinctly, always mindful of the effect my words have on and within the organization. I also recognize that, as a Woman of Color, I may be viewed differently by my peers of other ethnicities.[7] Therefore, the standards by which I may be judged are different from those of my white counterparts. This is also true, to some degree, for being a woman CEO; our spotlight is either brighter or dimmer, depending on who is looking.

Lesson #19: Rock Star Treatment

Along with the awareness of the spotlight of leadership came the fact that as I climbed the professional ladder, people began to treat me differently, especially when I attained the level of CEO.

I distinctly recall becoming a vice president. I was thrilled that I had attained a position one rung below CEO; however, I had not anticipated how starstruck other employees at that organization were by the title. I remember walking around and introducing myself to staff. I also went so far as volunteering to shadow frontline employees

---

[7] We have a saying in the Black community that we must "work twice as hard to get half as much."

to better understand the organization from multiple perspectives so that I could place my role in context. But on one occasion, a security guard asked me why I was shadowing employees, because I was a vice president and "they don't do that." I learned that the other vice presidents—five white males—had limited interaction with the staff, so my actions were seen as strange and caused a distinction to be made between the other VPs and me. To maintain my fledgling position within the rank of my peers, I had to stop my shadowing activities.

While this move helped normalize my relations with the other vice presidents, it left a sour taste in my mouth that the line of demarcation between me and coworkers whose titles were below mine was as strong as it was and was an important cultural component of the organization. I tried to change this part of the culture with only limited success. I chose instead to regularly walk around the organization and learn about and interact with frontline staff. They appreciated that I cared enough to speak and laugh with them, and I believe it made me a stronger leader.

Attaining the title of CEO was a greater adjustment for me because my employees treated me like a rock star—wanted to speak with me and spend time with me. In some cases, employees asked to touch me, and several asked for my autograph! It was surreal and very humbling.

In moments like these, I am reminded of my encounter with Dr. Maya Angelou, one of my favorite poets, who wrote a poem titled "Phenomenal Woman." I met her in California at a hotel. As I walked toward the registration desk, Dr. Angelou was walking toward the exit. I spoke and apologized for interrupting her and told her that I was a fan of her work. She graciously extended her hand, asked my name, and thanked me for stopping and sharing my words with her. I felt as though I had an audience with a queen! I remember how she made me feel—that she saw me and valued me without knowing me. She embodied one of her most often-quoted sayings, "People will forget what you said, people will forget what you did, but people will never forget how you made them feel." I adopted that credo and attempt to model it with my staff—I want them to know that I see them and value their contributions to our organization and those we serve—and anyone I encounter in my life journey.

I also eventually recognized that my presence in the room changes the atmosphere, for good or for bad depending on the topic.

In my opinion, Dr. Angelou's lesson has allowed me to develop a reputation as a caring, compassionate leader who, while mindful of my rock-star status, attempts to share the starlight with staff.

Lesson #20: Learning to Appreciate the Journey While Never Losing Sight of the Destination

As CEO, I am responsible for setting the vision for the organization consistent with its mission and making progress toward that goal. Consequently, I am always living with tension between celebrating our successes and never losing sight of our goals.

On occasion, this has been a difficult balance because, as the leader, I am required to show sincere appreciation for our employees' efforts on behalf of our clients (having instituted a new culture of positive reinforcement) while reminding each that we have more to do before we can rest on our laurels. This balance is especially hard as a change agent because I have an internal checklist of things I would like to see accomplished during my limited time in the organization, so I focus not so much on what we have done as on what is left to do. This has been a point of contention with my leadership team, which has counseled me to spend more time acknowledging and thanking our staff when every instinct is telling me that we can and must do more.

This lesson, again, is a work in progress for me.

LESSON #21: TOTAL DELEGATION VERSUS TOTAL CONTROL

I recognized early in my career that I need autonomy to do my best work. I need to be allowed room to get the work done. I do not work well with a supervisor who micromanages me.

Consequently, I adopted the style of giving the people who report to me directly, especially my leadership team, full responsibility for managing their areas. This means that they are fully responsible and accountable for what happens in their divisions. To my way of thinking, those on my team each own a piece of the agency's "business" and are the CEO of that portion of the business; they are responsible for tracking their transactions (finances), managing their staff (human resources), and producing, delivering, and assessing their product line (programs and services). I equally expect that, when I ask for information or provide direction, they will respond and provide me with timely reports on their divisions' operations, including challenges and solutions when issues arise.

However, even though I believe in full delegation, there are times when I must step in. Sometimes information that I have requested has not been forthcoming or decisions that I believed should have been made were not and caused other challenges that required my input or resolution. In general, I attempt to afford my team time to complete their tasks or an opportunity to provide me feedback regarding what I have asked of them, but there have been times when I have taken the reins from one of my team to accomplish a goal I believed to be necessary for the agency's success.

For example, one division underspent its grant funds several years in a row. When its leaders were asked to explain, the response was usually that they had fewer employees than were budgeted for; however, the number of vacancies did not account for the amount underspent. So, after two years of significant dollars returned to the funder and conversations with the division head about better managing funds, I decided to create a position and fill it with a current staff member. I discussed the issue with the head of the division prior to implementation, but the conversation primarily was a directive rather than a discussion. I am pleased to report that the position has given us greater control over those resources and we're in the process of refining the role further.

Another challenge for me is that, while I believe in total delegation, it sometimes conflicts with my need to get issues resolved quickly. This has resulted in my becoming frustrated with my team and vice versa because they require more time to resolve an issue that I think can be taken care of quickly and decisively.

I recently hired an executive coach, who is helping me work through my need for decisive and quick (whenever possible) resolutions to issues from my team when their personal styles may require a more thoughtful approach. As is often the case in a twelve-step program like Alcoholics Anonymous, acknowledging that I have a problem is an important first step!

LESSON #22: MAKING WHAT OTHERS CONSIDER HEAVEN YOUR PERSONAL HELL

At the beginning of the book, I shared that I am a Christian and that many of my life experiences have been influenced by my beliefs. I have tried to make decisions based on what I believe God is directing me to do at a particular time. This is especially true regarding my career choices. Consequently, God has led me to interesting careers, some of which I could not have anticipated. But unfortunately, there have been occasions when a position that I believed God wanted for me and that others expressed jealousy about turned into a nightmare.

I was privileged to work for a world-renowned cultural organization that was the finest of its type in the country. I was on the leadership team and enjoyed all the perks ascribed to the position and to the organization. For several years, I considered it a dream job and did not foresee any issues that would cause me to leave. However, my boss, with whom I had established an honest and mutually respectful relationship, eventually began questioning me based on comments from one of his leadership team members, who was my peer. As I established in lesson #6, I had formed a transparent relationship with my boss, whereby I kept him informed of my activities and shared my truths with him at every opportunity. I assumed that he understood me enough to know my character and that, if someone raised an issue with my performance, he would respond, "What does what you are sharing with me about her have to do with you performing your job?" instead of believing someone else's report. I was confronted by my boss four times based on my peer's reports, and each time, I confronted my colleague, asking for an explanation of his actions and requesting that I be given the courtesy of responding before he sought to speak with our boss about me. It never happened.

Subsequently, I lost respect for my boss and that colleague and became distracted at work. What I and others had considered to be a dream job was becoming a nightmare!

In hindsight, I should have recognized that the colleague reporting on me felt threatened because, prior to my arrival, he was the boss's go-to person. That changed when I was hired. Also, I should have been more reflective instead of allowing my self-doubt to determine how well I would manage. For example, I could have chosen to look at the multiple positives of the position—the higher level of leadership, the once-in-a-lifetime experiences, preparation for a C-suite position, wonderful colleagues with whom I enjoyed working, et cetera. Instead, I became quieter, allowed the situation to consume me, and subsequently forced myself to seek other employment.

LESSON #23: GROWTH IS REQUIRED

I have often heard people say that they have not changed over time, that they are the same person they always have been. I find that difficult to believe because, in my experience, change is a necessary part of growth. I recently purchased a sign that says, "No Regrets,

Just Lessons Learned." I have adopted this as one of my mantras because every experience, good or bad, is an opportunity to grow. And, as a leader, I have found change a necessary part of the job and the journey.

In lesson #4, I talked about the changes in perspective I experienced in different roles. While I detailed those changes, I glossed over the invaluable lessons that shaped me as a leader and the experiences I pursued to become a better leader.

Let me be clear: while my values have rarely changed (for example, open communication, honesty, and integrity), changes in my role required changes in myself. I learned to talk and walk with more authority because it was necessary to exude confidence and competence. This was accomplished by what has been called "taking up more space." Women in leadership must often adopt the style of men, who still hold most leadership positions in companies. So, to be competitive, I chose to do the following five things.

1. I modulated my voice so that I did not appear to ask a question when making a statement.
2. I sat at a table and spread my materials in front of me so that I filled my area.
3. I leaned into a discussion instead of sitting back or appearing to withdraw when I wanted to make a point or someone attempted to talk over or ignore me.
4. I stood with my feet planted, back straight, and eyes forward to reflect a confident demeanor and posture, using my five-foot-seven (five-foot-nine in heels) height as a tool to command respect.
5. I used eye contact in every communication, especially with men.

I also make a concerted effort to seek opportunities to increase my knowledge and to develop the skills I need to succeed in my personal life and at work. President John F. Kennedy is quoted as having said, "Leadership and learning are indispensable to each other." I agree!

One of the important ways to grow is by having a mentor and mentoring someone. I have been privileged to be mentored by several wonderful people over the years. Some mentored me without knowing they were because I became a student of watching them lead. Others were formal mentors I pursued or who pursued me because we each saw something in the other that we wanted to nurture or to grow from because of our interactions. There are books on mentorship, so I will not go into detail about that here, but I will state that every encounter was an opportunity to learn what to do and what not to do when (or if) I became a leader. And, as I mentioned in my introduction, I have been intentional in understanding my leadership journey because of my personal need to know and the requirement that God has placed on my life to explain it to others.

I think it is safe to say that people who have known me for years are surprised by the changes I have made in how I "show up" in the world now. It is amazing, but also intentional.

LESSON #24: EXIT STRATEGY— KNOW WHEN IT IS TIME TO LEAVE

As a change agent, I am always mindful of the clock ticking on my tenure in any given place or role. My purpose is to leave an organization in better condition than when I arrived. This simply means that I must have an idea of what I want to accomplish, relatively speaking, at the time I first sit down behind the desk.

For me, leadership is a series of decisions that I make daily, including the decision to leave when I feel that I have accomplished what I wanted to accomplish or what I was able to accomplish given the circumstances.

I have found that I become restless in a job when I can "name that tune in one note."[8] However, I need to interject that, as a Christian, I may desire to leave an organization or pursue a new role, but God has sometimes told me to wait. This has been frustrating when I believed I had completed my mental list of goals I set for myself or those that were set for me by my boss and I was struggling to stay engaged in the work. That frustration with waiting on God once caused me to actively seek a job that turned out to be one of the worst experiences of my life. Now I know to wait for God's direction, however long He takes.

Once I learned to surrender my will for my career to God, the wait, while still difficult, had purpose. Every job I have obtained over the last twenty-five years has been a divine move of God. I have learned to pay attention to signs or cues that a change is about to occur and to get ready.

To a certain degree, I keep the knowledge that there will be an exit at some point in the back of my mind to prevent myself from making my leadership position in an organization my personal fiefdom. Unfortunately, I have met many people who built their identity around their position and lost themselves in the process. Every person in an organization, including the CEO, is dispensable. As soon as I understood that, it became easier for me to recognize when the curtain was beginning to close and I needed to prepare to exit stage right or left.

Lesson #25: Forgetting Where You Come From

I am not certain how often people are reminded, "Never forget where you came from." Others reminded me of this off and on as I pursued higher education and, later, increasing responsibilities and higher salaries at work.

---

[8] This is a reference to a game show that began in the 1950s and has recently been resurrected. The show's host asks contestants to identify a specific song based on notes played on a musical instrument. The winning contestant is the one who identifies the song by the fewest notes.

The first time I became aware of this issue was on one of my visits home from college. I think I was sharing something I learned with my mother, and she uttered this phrase. Looking back, I am fairly certain that I was trying to impress her with my new knowledge; instead, I believe she saw it as my thinking that I was better than she was because I attended college and she hadn't. In hindsight, I was a little arrogant. However, I learned to temper my enthusiasm and tried to act as normal as possible at her house to reduce the tension I created by demonstrating a new me.

Unfortunately, as I have counseled other first-generation college students, there comes a point in your college career when you must decide to move on from your family's expectations that you not change, or you must change because your future depends on your becoming a different person. For me, this occurred between my sophomore and junior years. I felt that I could not move forward if I were too afraid to lose the support of my family. As I have explained this decision point to others, the same family and friends who cheered you on during your formative years can become your detractors as you continue your professional journey. It is hurtful when it happens, but it is a necessary part of the journey.

It comes down to a simple question: Will you stay who you have been—the person other people want you to remain—or will you give yourself permission to stretch and become the person necessary to the future you have envisioned for yourself? While the question is simple, the process is not.

I have learned to tell anyone who makes this statement to me that, while I remember the place from which I came, I am not trying to go back to it. The lessons are ever with me and have shaped the person I am now.

Lesson #26: Lifting as I Climb

It was interesting to learn that I am a double minority—both Black and female. That is the order in which I place both as I continue to live my life.

My primary filter is as a Black person in America, who has been taught that I must work twice as hard to earn half as much. For example, when I enter a room, I immediately begin looking for other Black people, regardless of gender. In television commercials, I look to see how diverse the actors are. The same is true for television shows or movies. I use the same lens when I see print advertisements. Also, I am consciously aware that the color of my skin may cause people who have already decided who I am to treat me differently, so I steel myself against the possibility of being discounted when I meet someone new professionally or I am in an unfamiliar environment.

However, a mentor of mine expanded my thinking beyond defining myself primarily in terms of my ethnicity. She said, "Jackie, have you considered that they [white males] may not mind your being Black, but they may have a problem with your being a female?" The question blew my mind—I had never considered the possibility that being female would take precedence over being Black in their minds! This was earth-shattering for me! *You mean that someone could discriminate against me because I am a woman and not because I am Black?!*

That mind shift helped solidify my commitment to the concept of lifting as I climb. This is a commitment to creating opportunities for other Blacks or People of Color, as well as women, whenever I am in a position to do so. It requires positioning these individuals to succeed or to look beyond where they are to where they could be with more education or experience and helping them attain one or the other, or both, as they climb.

This concept is not new; for generations, it has been the standard by which white men and many ethnic groups have succeeded. Women have seen a significant rise in the occupation of key leadership roles over the past twenty years. In fact, there are now more women attending college than men for the first time in American history.

This bodes well for the future. Additionally, more People of Color are in college than ever before, especially Blacks and Latinos, but on a much smaller scale. Unfortunately, while these groups have made progress, this progress continues to lag significantly behind that of white females.

I am hopeful that things will continue to improve. But either way, as long as I sit in a leadership seat, so to speak, I will ensure that People of Color and women have seats next to me or are, at a minimum, in the room!

Throughout the book, I've shared my journey and my insights gained from those experiences. I've introduced the concept of culture as not only my research interest but also an important filter in my professional life.

When we think of individuals and organizations, we primarily think of the cultural norms—customs, traditions, language, and behaviors—that members take for granted. These norms are passed down from parents to children, from group member to new member, and from companies to new employees and provide the rules by which members are expected to conform and comply.

What has been missing is an understanding of the often-unconscious cultural aspects of leadership. Leadership development is more than learning the organizational culture, which has been the primary discussion in leadership development; it's also recognizing the cultural nuances the individual presents with and confronts when they assume a leadership role.

Chapter 5

The Culture in Leadership— Professional Leadership Role Formation

As I previously noted, I earned my doctorate in psychological anthropology studying the transition of high school students to college. My research interest later became a larger and more complex one: the process all people go through acquiring cultural knowledge when transitioning to a new role, and its effects on success in the role and on self-identity.

In 2009, I developed a theory of leadership that describes the unconscious cultural knowledge that someone in a new role must possess. And in 2019, I expanded the discussion to what I call the *leadership orbit*, which details the changes in perspective that result from acquiring increasing leadership responsibilities and their connections to traits inherent within a leadership role. I described this in lesson #4. As this is a theory, it is important to understand its theoretical origins.

As I previously defined it, culture includes the taken-for-granted rules of engagement for a group and its customs, traditions, language, and behaviors. Because they are part of the normal ways people are expected to think or act, these behaviors are usually unconscious once learned.

During my doctoral research, an idea began to form regarding culture and its part in transitioning from one role to another, which later expanded to transitioning from one leadership role to another. This idea was sparked by the question, "During freshman year, how is the culturally constructed identity of 'college student' a factor in the successful transition of students from high school to college as a result of their socialization to this new social status or role?" The theoretical basis for the study was Victor Turner's rites of passage (1964). Turner theorized three phases. Phase 1, separation, includes symbolic behavior denoting a detachment of the individual from an earlier fixed point in the social structure (that is, a "state"). In phase 2, the liminal period, the individual's state is considered ambiguous: the old state is gone, but the individual has not assumed a new state yet. Phase 3, aggregation, signifies completion of the process.

I identified six concurrent steps in the development of the college student identity.

1. Students' primary identity is "smart and intelligent," which made this college appealing to them.
2. Independence from their parents and personal responsibility for their actions and activities assist students in developing a college identity.

3. Students have the freedom to make choices that were not available to them prior to college, and the consequences of those choices are their responsibilities.

4. Making new friends is critical to adjusting to college because it is primarily through these relationships that students are socialized to the college's cultural environment.

5. Time management and development of study skills are important to students' academic and social success at the college.

6. Students are able to learn about themselves by revisiting their pre-college identities in a new sociocultural environment that values diversity of thought and expression.

As a result of my study, I began to wonder what influence, if any, self-identity and cultural acquisition have on a person's successful transition from one professional role to another. Several questions formed in my mind: *How does a person assuming leadership learn the new role? It is often stated that you need to bring your whole self to the work environment. What does that mean? As a leader, are you required to change who you are? If so, in what ways?* and *Who must you be to be successful in the new role?*

These questions led me to identify three kinds of culture that influence a leader: (1) organizational culture, (2) personal culture, and (3) positional culture.

Organizational Culture

Organizational culture, as defined by the shared values and expectations within an organization, has become a major focus of management and leadership books and consulting services in the twenty-first century. The origin of the term can be traced to a book by Dr. Elliott Jaques titled *The Changing Culture of a Factory*, written in 1951. Dr. Jaques's theory was based on his study of a publicly held British company that was primarily engaged in the manufacture, sale, and servicing of metal bearings. He focused his inquiry on the description, analysis, and development of corporate group behaviors. According to Dr. Jaques, "the culture of the factory is its customary and traditional way of thinking and doing of things, which is shared to a greater or lesser degree by all its members, and which new members must learn, and at least partially accept, in order to be accepted into service in the firm."[9]

PERSONAL CULTURE

Personal culture includes personal markers such as gender identity, age, ethnicity, and sexual orientation, to name a few. These are the first filters through which an individual views their new role. For example, as a self-described Black, heterosexual, sixty-plus-year-old female, I have a view of the world that has been shaped by the experience of each one of these markers. When I interviewed for a position, acquired it, and operated within it, I viewed—and continue to view—my experience through these lenses. However, I did not

---

[9] Jaques, Elliott. *The Changing Culture of a Factory*. London: Tavistock Publications, 1951: 251.

become aware of using them as filters until a few years ago because they are often unconscious.

Ethnicity instead of Race

Ethnicity and *race* are different social constructs, but these terms have been used interchangeably for decades. Race has been theorized to exist for centuries—that is, early scientists theorized that there were different races of people. This theory was taught and believed to be true and has been the cornerstone of racist policies around the world. However, race does not exist in nature. After hundreds of years of research to prove its existence, science has proven that there is only the human race. Consequently, it is now widely agreed that race is not a biological reality. The construct of race has evolved to a new understanding that the issue is not race but ethnicity, which includes the customs and traditions associated with a social group of people who have a common national or cultural identity.

My cultural affiliation or ethnicity determines to a significant degree how I present me to myself and to others daily. It is also a filter other people use in how they perceive me.

Gender

Gender has commonly been defined to encompass two sexes (male and female), especially when considered with reference to social and cultural differences rather than biological ones. The term has expanded to include the terms *transgender, non-conforming, queer, intersex,* and many more that do not correspond to established ideas of male and female.

Commonly held beliefs have suggested that the genders are different—that people often think and act differently due to socialization based on gender roles in their culture or brain development differences depending on their reproductive organs. However, much of what the world has believed to be true regarding male and female is undergoing a significant shift with broader acknowledgment of transgender, nonbinary, and pangender identities.

Age

While age is a biological reality, it is also a social construct, meaning that each culture defines age for members of its group. Consequently, societies have different expectations as to what a person of a certain age can or should do. These expectations vary across cultures and affect how people view themselves in space and in time. For example, in the United States, fifty-year-old people are not expected to act as if they were in their twenties; instead, they are expected not only to act differently but to think and behave differently. This is cultural.

Sexual Orientation

Sexual orientation is a fairly new topic of discussion, but not a new issue. Only since the sexual revolution of the 1960s, the devastating effects of the AIDS epidemic on the LGBTQIA (lesbian, gay, bisexual, transgender, queer, intersex, and asexual) community, and other equally significant events have sexual orientation—and its effect on how people define themselves or how others define them—been a topic that can be discussed openly. The LGBTQIA community, which for many years was forced to remain hidden because of stigma, has become more visible and acknowledged. Sexual orientation, too, is cultural and an important filter.

Personal cultural factors, as I have defined them, are the first filters we use when we are introduced to a new role, including leadership.[10] They help us make sense of the roles we inhabit and how we choose to occupy them. In the following figure, I represent personal culture graphically overlaid on the role we inhabit.

---

[10] While not on the graph, socioeconomic status, which is cultural, is another lens through which people organize and define themselves.

Positional Culture

I define *positional culture* as traits that are ascribed to the individual roles within an organization regardless of their level. Positional culture includes the cultural markers of language associated with a particular field or role, appropriate clothing for the role, behavior expected in the role, and the social niche available to or required or expected within the role.

Positional culture also includes traits associated with any role, such as the accountability, authority, expectations, power, responsibilities, and status ascribed to the position or role.

Each of these will be explained in greater detail.

Cultural Markers

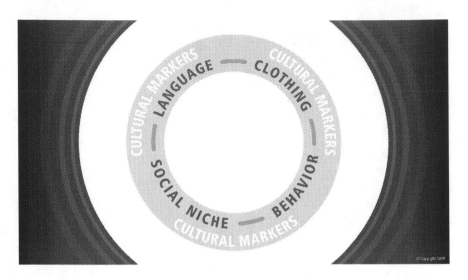

Cultural markers are associated with having a role or, more specifically, learning and inhabiting it. Every role has certain characteristics associated with it. As noted above, these include language, clothing, behavior, and development of or interaction within a social niche.

Language

Any organization has language that is particular to the enterprise it is operating within. For example, when I was an undergraduate student, I had to learn the terminology of college, such as *drop/add, pass/fail, registrar, professor, lecturer,* and many other terms used in the college culture. Wall Street has a jargon all its own. So do the medical field, the U.S. government, and law enforcement. However, each role within a particular enterprise, especially a leadership role, also has a language, one that must be learned to fulfill the role successfully.

In lesson #15, I talked about the *we* in leadership and the *I* in falling short, but there is much more to it than that. As a leader, my language matters—the words I use and how I use them are a direct reflection of my workplace. My words have the power to elevate the organization, an employee, or a client, or they can equally tear down each one. Consequently, leaders must understand the need to be careful about sharing random thoughts or negative musings because, as I noted in lesson #18, people are always watching, and by extension, they are always listening.

Additionally, there is an expectation that a leader will speak with authority. A person can quickly lose credibility if they appear to be confused and indecisive. This does not mean that you must always have the answer to every problem, but it does mean that your language must demonstrate you are in control of the situation and are working on a resolution, even though you may not have the solution yet.

Your language can move the organization forward or hinder its progress, so be aware of the effect it can have at whatever level you occupy.

Clothing

You can often tell what level a person occupies within an organization by their clothes. For example, when I worked in a hospital, I could distinguish the doctors from the nurses and orderlies from technicians because of their uniforms. This is also true in other types of organizations.

When I began my leadership climb, I worked primarily with undergraduate students and was expected to dress in a manner that made me seem accessible to an eighteen- or twenty-two-year-old. My clothing was comfortable but could not include casual pieces like jeans and T-shirts. When I became a director with staff to supervise, I began to wear more structured shirts, skirts, and slacks with jackets and unassuming jewelry. In this way, I was always prepared, as I was coached by my mentors, to attend unexpected meetings at any time. They told me that, in addition to dressing for my current role, I should dress for the part I wanted because, again, someone was always watching! This recommendation has been invaluable to me in my career.

I would be remiss, though, if I did not mention that my personal style has evolved over the years. While I adopted a corporate look when I became a director and continued it as a vice president, I learned to adapt the expectations others had of me with my personal twist. For example, when I worked in a music museum, I often wore business suits paired with stylish shoes or statement earrings and necklaces. I felt that I was dressing for the part I had (museum executive) while preparing for the part I wanted (CEO).

Now as a CEO, I maintain my unique way of dressing, but also I recognize the need to wear more traditional clothes when attending meetings with other CEOs or when representing the agency to the public.

Behavior

The higher you go on the leadership ladder, the more you will probably hear the saying, "Don't do anything your mother won't be proud of" or "Don't do anything that may make the six o'clock news." Your behavior as a leader will reflect well or poorly on the organization.

Because you have the spotlight, everything you do and the way you behave are dissected by friend and foe. For example, I don't have the luxury of ignoring a staff member in the hall; I am always expected to acknowledge and engage with staff because it matters to them that I "see" them—that by my speech and mannerisms, they know that I value their contributions. Unfortunately, recognizing staff can be positive and negative. When you appear to favor someone, it is a problem, and when you do not, it is also a problem. Consequently, as CEO, I have developed a delicate dance with staff in which I try to recognize their humanity and contributions to our organization without appearing to favor anyone in my interactions.

With those outside my organization, my behavior as CEO must be collegial, yet firm. I must communicate my mastery of my organization through my authoritative language and my posture. I am expected to look and act the part of a chief executive. In fact, I have developed a trick that I play when I attend a meeting or event where I may know few people—in my mind, I place a crown on my head, straighten my shoulders, and walk as if I am regal. I have been told that my carriage causes people to want to know me because I appear to be a person of interest!

Social Niche

You will recall I found in my research that developing a social niche or friendship network is an important step in a student's successful transition to college. This is equally true at every level of leadership because social niche development influences your decisions regarding the people with whom you interact and the advice you receive.

There is a fraternity or sorority among CEOs. I believe it is due to our collective understanding of the enormity of the job. Consequently, we CEOs look to each other for counsel and support. I distinctly recall a time when I realized that I was no longer a member of my professional group because I had attained a title that set me apart from those with whom I had developed great relationships but whose title and responsibilities were now different than mine. Unfortunately, my change in status changed our interactions and our conversations because these people were uncomfortable with my inability to share information as I had in the past and the evolving perspective required of me in my new role. Consequently, we drifted apart, and I developed other relationships at the new level.

This need to develop and navigate a new social niche when you assume a new role is not unique, but it is seldom discussed.

Jacklyn A. Chisholm Ph.D.

Simultaneous Cultural Learning

We have so far explored personal and cultural markers that are operating simultaneously as you assume a new position. This can be represented graphically as the following diagram.

This diagram illustrates that, as you assume a new role with personal markers as filters (age, gender, ethnicity, sexual orientation, and socioeconomic status), you are also assuming the cultural markers associated with the role (language, clothing, behavior, and social niche). And you are required to learn and adapt to them to competently perform the role.

Role Traits

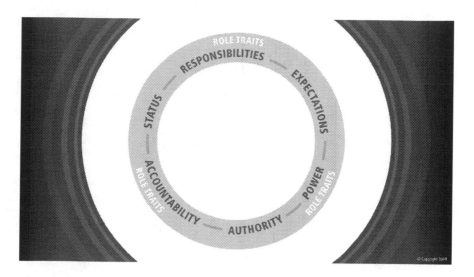

Each professional role you occupy has certain traits or characteristics associated with it. These include the position's status, responsibilities, expectations, power, authority, and accountability. I assume that we are all acquainted with these terms, but just to establish a baseline understanding of each, I will define them.

- **Status:** A role's status is defined by where the role sits within the hierarchy of the organization. The higher a role is in the hierarchy, the more status is ascribed to it. This is also true of a person's position relative to the seat of power within an organization. A person with the CEO's ear will have a higher status relative to those who do not.
- **Responsibilities:** Roles within organizations are usually centered on written job descriptions. These descriptions detail the responsibilities assigned to the roles, by which the people occupying the roles will be evaluated.
- **Expectations:** While a job description details the responsibilities associated with a role, expectations regarding successfully performing the role are usually determined by

the supervisor or the board of directors in the case of the CEO, or by the person inhabiting the role if they have set higher expectations for themselves than their supervisor has.

- **Power:** Each role has some agency or positional power associated with it. Without positional power, the people occupying the roles would have to draw on their individual characteristics or abilities to influence others (that is, personal power) to perform the roles successfully.
- **Authority:** As with power, a given amount of authority is ascribed to each role in an organization in order for you to perform the work or, if you are a supervisor, to have others perform the work that you delegate to them and are accountable for.
- **Accountability:** Being accountable is often thought of as interchangeable with being responsible, but accountability encompasses not only your personal actions but also those of the people who report to you.

The board of directors established my responsibilities as the CEO (as detailed in my job description) and set the job expectations by which I am evaluated annually; my status, power, and authority are communicated to the staff and others by my title of CEO, which is the highest administrative title in the organization; and I am ultimately responsible and accountable for every aspect of the organization I lead.

The role traits and the cultural markers of your position are learned simultaneously and filtered through your personal markers. All of this occurs unconsciously and may be associated with your feeling overwhelmed without knowing the source of the anxiety. Your mind works to make sense of all the information it is receiving simultaneously while you are usually unaware that this is happening in the background.

This is represented graphically as the following.

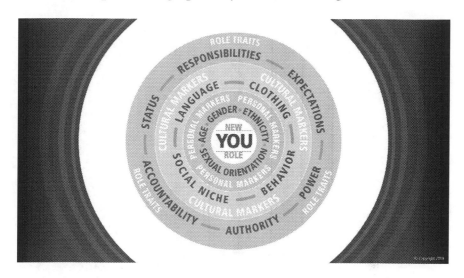

The final unconscious cultural knowledge is the change in self-identity that occurs when learning a new professional role. For much of the book, I have primarily focused on the role of leadership, but this is true for any new role undertaken willingly or at someone else's insistence. This, too, is cultural and is influenced by our prior personal and professional experiences.

SELF-IDENTITY

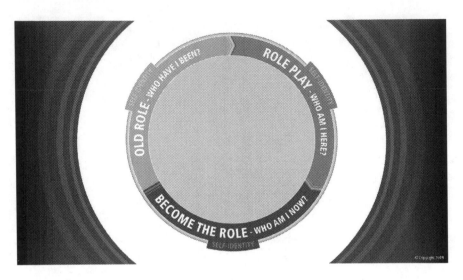

As with Victor Turner's rites of passage theory, I have identified three phases of the transition from the old role to the new role and the self-questions associated with each.

Phase 1: Role Separation—Who Have I Been?

I have always been fairly ambitious. I wanted to get straight As in school, to be the first to graduate from college, and to be the first to accomplish great things for myself and by extension for my family. So I made a conscious decision to constantly strive for better, especially in my career. Consequently, I sought opportunities to advance and was privileged to climb higher until I became CEO of a large nonprofit.

Each change in role required that I leave my old identity behind to accept a new one. However, most of us, myself included, think only in terms of acquiring a new title with increased responsibility and money. My experience suggests that a role change is more than that. Transitioning to a new role also required an identity shift—leaving behind how I defined myself before I accepted the new position.

The decision to apply for ever-increasing responsibilities, titles, and money was the beginning of my role separation because I had to first entertain the notion of leaving where I was prior to seeking another job. (Role separation also occurs for people who are promoted without having to apply for a new position. However, in this case, transitions may be more challenging because individuals who were once peers may try to diminish your accomplishments to keep you at the level they are used to you operating at with them.)

As I recounted previously, I clearly remember when I decided that the next position in my career would be CEO: More than once, I had been blamed for things I had not done. In that moment, I decided that if I was going to be blamed anyway, I might as well be in charge! That moment caused a shift in me; I shifted from identifying myself as a vice president to identifying myself as a future CEO and pursued it relentlessly.

Phase 2: Role Play—Who Am I Here?

I call this the "fake it till you make it" phase because at this point, I had been hired as chief executive, and everyone I met treated me as if I were a fully functioning CEO when, in fact, I was trying to figure out how to operate within the role.

During this phase, I spent a great deal of time observing others and watching for subtle clues as to how I was supposed to act toward staff and how they viewed the role of CEO within the organization and me as the new CEO. I also quickly interviewed my direct reports and asked specific questions to help me learn the organizational culture as they understood it, as well as the previous CEO's administration and activities.

Additionally, I sought to identify the gaps I could fill to help the organization's renaissance through knowing myself to be:

- A change agent, who enjoys bringing order to chaos by reimagining processes and procedures to increase efficiency
- A servant leader, who believes in compassionate, mission-driven activities; who acknowledges and celebrates the value of and contribution of each employee; who honors our organization's responsibility to our clients and stakeholders and recognizes that nonprofit is a tax status, not a business strategy (We are first a charitable business that requires we be reputable stewards of the funds entrusted to us.)
- A psychological anthropologist, who understands that culture drives the processes and procedures of all organizations

I admit to reading the books *How to Think like a CEO* and *The Virtual Executive: How to Act like a CEO Online and Offline* by Debra A. Benton, who interviewed hundreds of CEOs to distill traits she considers important for getting to and staying in the top position. Her books are very insightful, but after having been in my role for a few years, I realized what is missing from them is it is okay to pretend for a period of time to know what a CEO is and how one needs to comport oneself. One day, when I least expected it, I would no longer have to play the role because I had, over time, come to fully inhabit it. Another way of saying this is that I "became" the role instead of performing it—the difference being ownership. I eventually owned the job because I grew to instinctively know what being a CEO meant to me and how I would operate. Once this happened, I rarely second-guessed my decisions or my actions because I had developed my vision for the organization, a plan to move us forward, and the rules of engagement for the role to make my vision a reality.

Phase 3: Role Integration—Who Am I Now?

For a short time, I was privileged to lead a start-up music museum as CEO. I was responsible for creating the board of directors, developing the articles of incorporation, and writing a business plan.

In fact, I considered myself the "CEO of air" because the museum was a concept and not a reality yet. So while I had decent knowledge of a music museum's inner workings because of my previous experience, I was not certain at that point that I knew enough to be successful.

This all changed during a meeting with the local chamber of commerce. The president discussed start-up nonprofit issues that are often overlooked. As he recited each issue, I thought, *I know that, and I know that, and I know that.* At the end of his comments, I responded, "This is how we did it at …" and addressed each issue in detail. In that moment, I realized that I truly owned the CEO role even though the museum was still in the conceptualization stage.

In my current role, because I was conscious of the three phases in role formation (role separation, role play, and role integration), I monitored my progress through each stage. I knew that I would spend some time shifting from my previous identity to that of CEO of a large nonprofit, and that to fake it till I made it was an important phase in the process. However, I was uncertain how long it would be before I fully inhabited the role. This occurred, unfortunately, through a crisis within the organization.

I thought I would have at least six months to one year to understand the organization and to get comfortable in the role. However, within three months of my arrival, the organization's largest grant was in jeopardy. This meant that I had to fast-track my learning curve and get into the details to address the issue quickly. I also had to allay staff fears that I would need to lay off hundreds of employees. At the end of a seven-month process to correct organizational mistakes, the funding was successfully retained, and I integrated my role as CEO into my identity. That process required me to move from playing the role to being the role.

I should pause and say that moving from phase 2 to phase 3—from role play to role integration—is often catalyzed by a crisis that requires an all-in response. This was true for me during that period of uncertainty.

Once role integration took place, I found it easier to operate as CEO without taking cues from employees regarding their definitions of the role, monitoring my behavior to determine if I was playing the role correctly, or second-guessing my decisions. Also, while my behavior toward staff did not change, my relationship to who I had been prior to becoming CEO did. I was more confident and less anxious about doing a good job. When I said to myself, "I got this!" I believed it! That was when I knew the journey to integration was finally over.

These changes in self-identity, like the other concepts in chapter 5 occur simultaneously and in the background, like the workings of an operating system in a computer. They shape our perceptions of ourselves and the roles we inhabit, and the expectations others have for us in those roles. This is represented graphically as the following.

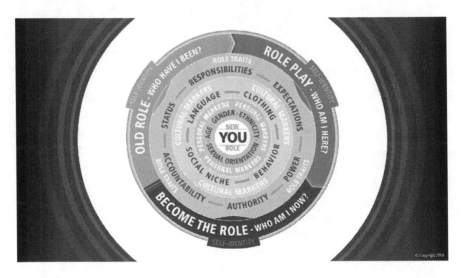

Chapter 5 acknowledges that a new leadership role requires more than learning new responsibilities (and the organizational culture, if you are joining a new organization). It also requires recognizing the following.

- Your personal culture is the initial filter through which you will experience the new role.
- Positional culture associated with the new role (cultural markers, role traits, and self-identity) also has an effect on leadership success.

- There will be a time of faking it till you make it as you learn these things on the way to becoming fully integrated in the role. It's an expected and necessary part of the process.
- Most importantly, all the learning as the leader happens simultaneously. This often makes you feel overwhelmed by the experience without knowing the source of the anxiety.

Conclusion

The Journey Continues

I have come to the end of the book, but not the end of the lessons on my leadership journey.

My desire at the beginning of my writing was that my experiences and lessons motivate you to pursue all you are capable of and all God has for you, and that they inspire you to pursue leadership.[11] I hope that I have accomplished both.

All journeys have a beginning, a middle, and an end. Leadership is no different. During each phase in my journey, I learned invaluable lessons that I believe have enhanced me as a leader, including the painful experiences that, while instructive, I hope never to experience again!

The question remains as to whether leaders are born or made. I personally think that it can be a little of both. In my experience, others saw something in me that I didn't see in myself, and they were willing to nurture it in me. But I also had to be willing to pursue leadership positions and the necessary training—formal and informal—that would increase my likelihood of success.

When I look back on my life, I recognize that important choices I made in certain moments could have resulted in my being a battered wife and mother, dying due to suicide, or getting stuck in unfulfilling

---

[11] The latter is a worthwhile goal. We need individuals in our leadership ranks who understand leadership's awesome responsibilities as well as its realities.

jobs because I was too afraid to risk failure. I am not unique in that regard. All of us are on our different roads that eventually lead to a crossroad. One direction requires little effort; we are familiar with it and have a decent expectation of what will happen. The other is the road less traveled,[12] which has risk and the potential of greater reward. Depending on where we are in life, we may choose to stay on the safer road because we don't want the disruption that may accompany a different choice. However, the pull to leadership, as I described in chapter 3 on levels of leadership, often compelled me to take the more difficult road, not because I don't appreciate the status quo on occasion but because I have a need to go further, to be productive, and to make a difference.

One of my mantras is, "If an A is possible, I want an A+!" I'm not sure if this was forged in me due to my mother's labeling me the "smart one" or if it is innate. Either way, it is a value to which I ascribe. The way it has shown up in my life is that I am rarely satisfied with attaining mediocrity or doing things in a less-than-adequate way. Unfortunately, this drives my husband insane, but it has been very useful to me because it requires that I strive to perform to the best of my ability in whatever I undertake. Another downside to this is that I'm never fully comfortable because, while I may have had significant success in my job, I rarely stop to appreciate what has been accomplished because I'm always focused on what else needs to be done. I continue to work on finding a balance between the two extremes, especially when I am blinded to all that my staff have achieved and the need to celebrate and acknowledge their successes.

Good leaders must recognize their strengths and their weaknesses because their strengths will get them the job, but their weaknesses could cost them the job. It is often said that we must either seek training for our weaknesses or staff to them, meaning we hire people who complement us in the areas where we consider ourselves weak. It took me years to realize that I didn't need to know how to do

---

[12] M. Scott Peck's *The Road Less Traveled* was first published in 1978.

everything well, but I needed to fill whatever gaps I had through training or hiring well.

One caveat, though: there are certain skills as a CEO that you must have. These include understanding and successfully managing the finances of your organization and committing to developing your organization, yourself, and your staff in service of your clients. In my humble opinion, any leader with these skills will do well.

The insights and lessons that I've shared with you have been garnered over sixty years (with more in the future, I hope). Each has cost me something. Decisions were made—some good, some bad—and sacrifices were required, including with whom I would walk or run on my journey. While those of us who have attained the C-suite worked hard to get here, if we are honest with ourselves, we know we did not get here just by our effort. In my case, so many people were involved in my climb, and each contributed to my achieving what many leaders want—to be a CEO.

From my earliest days in my dysfunctional family and relationships to my restart personally and professionally because of bad decisions, to my eventual move out of darkness and into the life I am blessed to have now, I had to keep putting one foot in front of the other until I reached my goals. One of my favorite quotes is by Calvin Coolidge, the thirtieth president of the United States:

> Nothing in this world can take the place of persistence. Talent will not; nothing is more common than unsuccessful men with talent. Genius will not; unrewarded genius is almost a proverb. Education will not; the world is full of educated derelicts. Persistence and determination alone are omnipotent.

The road to leadership, like many things, is a marathon and not a sprint, and thank God that's the case. Every twist and turn that I've taken, I believe, prepared me for the monumental, awesome, and sometimes overwhelming responsibilities of leading a hundred-million-dollar organization with over four hundred employees who depend on our board's, my team's, and my decision making. Because I am the leader of the organization, I am able to give directives to staff and expect those directives to be carried out without delay, but I must also be cognizant of the interplay among my behavior; my communication style with the board, staff, clients, and key stakeholders; and the decisions I make on behalf of the organization.

As CEO, I must have deep knowledge of our finances and enough knowledge of our programs and services to understand them and to explain them to others. However, I don't need to understand every process and procedure in providing the services; that's the responsibility of my leadership team. My primary roles include visionary, implementer, fundraiser, mentor, role model, and cheerleader, which carry equal weight in their execution.

As I've recounted, I consider myself extremely blessed to have had the experiences that I've shared with you and the hard-won lessons that have shaped me as a leader. I would be remiss, however, if I didn't also share some of the resources that I've used throughout my career from authors I respect. This list is not exhaustive, but it includes those resources that were particularly meaningful to me.

- Babcock, Linda, and Sara Laschever. *Women Don't Ask: The High Cost of Avoiding Negotiation—and Positive Strategies for Change.* New York: Bantam Books, 2007.
- Blanchard, Kenneth, and Spencer Johnson. *The One Minute Manager.* New York: William Morrow, 1982.
- Blanchard, Kenneth, and Norman Vincent Peale. *The Power of Ethical Management.* New York: William Morrow, 1988.
- Brooks, Donna, and Lynne Brooks. *Seven Secrets of Successful Women.* New York: McGraw-Hill, 1997.
- Buckingham, Marcus. *First, Break All the Rules: What the World's Greatest Managers Do Differently.* New York: Gallup Press, 2016.
- Buckingham, Marcus, and Donald O. Clifton. *Now, Discover Your Strengths.* New York: Free Press, 2001.

- Carnegie, Dale. *How to Win Friends and Influence People*. New York: Pocket Books, 1998.
- Collins, Jim. *Good to Great: Why Some Companies Make the Leap ... and Others Don't*. New York: HarperBusiness, 2001.
- Covey, Stephen R. *The Seven Habits of Highly Effective People: Restoring the Character Ethic*. New York: Simon & Schuster, 1989.
- Fenton, Richard, and Andrea Waltz. *Go for No!: Yes Is the Destination, No Is How You Get There*. Orlando, FL: Courage Crafters, 2010.
- Fulghum, Robert. *All I Really Need to Know I Learned in Kindergarten*. New York: Ballantine Books, 2004.
- Hoenig, Christopher. *Six Essential Secrets for Thinking on a New Level: Making Decisions and Getting Results*. New York: Basic Books, 2000.
- Jakes, T. D. *Reposition Yourself: Living Life without Limits*. New York: Atria Books, 2007.
- Johnson, Spencer. *Who Moved My Cheese?: An Amazing Way to Deal with Change in Your Work and in Your Life*. New York: Putnam, 1998.
- Kotter, John P. *Leading Change*. Boston: Harvard Business Review Press, 1996.
- Maxwell, John C. *Developing the Leader Within You*. Nashville, TN: Thomas Nelson, 1993.
- Maxwell, John C. *The 21 Irrefutable Laws of Leadership: Follow Them and People Will Follow You*. Nashville, TN: Thomas Nelson, 1998.
- Maxwell, John C. *Failing Forward: Turning Mistakes into Stepping-Stones for Success*. Nashville, TN: Thomas Nelson, 2000.
- Maxwell, John C. *How Successful People Think: Change Your Thinking, Change Your Life*. New York: Center Street, 2009.
- Maxwell, John C. *The Five Levels of Leadership: Proven Steps to Maximize Your Potential*. New York: Center Street, 2011.

- Rath, Tom, and Donald O. Clifton. *How Full Is Your Bucket? Positive Strategies for Work and Life.* New York: Gallup Press, 2004.
- Sandberg, Sheryl. *Lean In: Women, Work, and the Will to Lead.* New York: Knopf, 2013.
- Schwartz, David J. *The Magic of Thinking Big.* New York: Simon & Schuster, 1987.
- Sinek, Simon. *Start with Why: How Great Leaders Inspire Everyone to Take Action.* New York: Portfolio, 2009.
- Stephenson, Sean. *Get Off Your "But": How to End Self-Sabotage and Stand Up For Yourself.* New York: John Wiley & Sons, 2009.
- Walker, David J. *You Are Enough: Always Have Been … Always Will Be.* Camarillo, CA: DeVorss & Company, 2007.

Every journey begins with the first step. My steps have led me to the position of CEO of the largest agency of its type in Ohio! The lessons I've learned along the way have been invaluable to me, and I hope that, should you decide leadership is your calling, they will inspire and inform you. I wish you all the best on your journey!

About the Author

Jacklyn Chisholm, Ph.D. has over 30 years of experience in personal and professional development, strategic planning, and government and community relations. Dr. Chisholm is the Founder and President of It's Worth It Consulting, LLC. She also serves as the President and Chief Executive Officer of the largest Community Action Agency in Ohio with revenues of over $42 million annually. Prior to that she served as the Vice President of Strategic Planning and Institutional Relations at the Rock and Roll Hall of Fame.

Dr. Chisholm is the recipient of numerous awards including the YWCA Women of Achievement, Crain's Cleveland Business Women of Note, Women of Color Foundation ISIS Award, and Council on Education National TRIO Achiever.

She was admitted to Case Western Reserve University where, over the course of 20 years, earned three advanced degrees: a Bachelor of Arts in medical anthropology, a Master of Arts in psychological anthropology, and a doctorate in psychological anthropology with an emphasis in educational anthropology. In addition, she has earned an Executive Certificate in Nonprofit Leadership from Harvard University's John F. Kennedy School of Government, as well as certificates from Harvard Business School, Cornell University Johnson Graduate School of Management's Administrative Management Institute and University of Pennsylvania Wharton School of Business.

Her varied and challenging experiences as a student and an adult learner led her to establish It's Worth It Consulting, LLC, in 2001, which offers personal and professional development training, coaching, consultation, and to blog about her experiences at drjacklynchisholm.com.

Printed in the United States
by Baker & Taylor Publisher Services